THE
ABUNDANCE
EFFECT

THE ABUNDANCE EFFECT

How to Shift from a Life of Scarcity to a Life of Abundance

By
JUSTIN MORALES

Silver Torch Press
Beverly Hills, CA

The Abundance Effect: How to Shift from a Life of Scarcity to a Life of Abundance ©2017 by Justin Morales

Printed in the United States of America.

ISBN: 978-1-942707-61-5
Library of Congress Control Number: 2017953338

www.AbundanceEffect.com
Justin@TheAbundanceEffect.com

 Published by Silver Torch Press
www.SilverTorchPress.com
Jill@SilverTorchPress.com

Information provided in this book is for informational purposes only. This information is NOT intended as a substitute for the advice provided by your physician or other healthcare provider. Neither the author nor the publisher shall be liable or responsible for any loss or damage allegedly arising from any information or suggestion in this book.

DEDICATION

To my daughters, Haven and Arie. May you have true abundance in your lives.

To my parents, Cathy and Irv Morales, who engrained a strong work ethic and a foundation of faith in me. To my wife, Lindsay, who has always supported me no matter how crazy my ideas have been. You are my rock in good times and bad, and I am grateful to you.

And to all you entrepreneurs. May you achieve your goals.

ACKNOWLEDGMENTS

First, I want to thank God, for His blessings. My hope is that I can be a good steward of all that He has given me.

I thank my wife, Lindsay, for always believing in me. No matter how crazy my ideas seemed, you always had my back. I can't thank you enough for that. Your support has allowed me to take the offensive, knowing that win, lose, or draw, you were always behind me. Thank you for blessing us with our two beautiful daughters and for being such an example and leader to them. You have always put us first and set things you love aside to support those around you. You are truly a gift, and I'm grateful to and for you.

To my parents, Irv and Cathy Morales, thank you for your unconditional love. You are an amazing example of what a marriage should be. I'm eternally grateful for all that you have taught me and for the way you raised me. I aspire to be as good a parent to my children as you were to me. You have always supported me in whatever path I chose. I love you guys so much!

Thanks to my friend and mentor, Marshall Thurber, who has either formed or enhanced many of my ideas. You have given me so many wonderful gifts, and I'm very grateful.

Thanks to Mike and Rhonda Haun, my in laws. You have created the most beautiful human and shaped her into the person she is today. I am grateful for your generous hearts and for supporting us in our journey.

Thank you to John Bell, my spiritual mentor. You have taught me so much and have kept me grounded, even in some of the most difficult times. Your time and knowledge has been a true gift.

Thanks to Kate Guden, my office manager, also known as my "work wife," for keeping everything going while I'm running around. I appreciate how you put up with my craziness and always forge ahead without question. Not only are you great at what you do, but you are a great friend as well.

Thanks Haven and Arie for inspiring me to be a better person and the best parent I can be.

Thanks to those who have contributed to this book, Hazel, Bonnie, and everyone who helped edit and read this behind the scenes, especially Paige Rabon. You guys are rock stars. I couldn't have done this without you.

TABLE OF CONTENTS

INTRODUCTION 1

CHAPTER ONE   EMOTIONAL ABUNDANCE 5

CHAPTER TWO   THE ABUNDANT MINDSET 30

CHAPTER THREE   RELATIONSHIP ABUNDANCE 53

CHAPTER FOUR   ABUNDANT VISION 76

CHAPTER FIVE   ABUNDANT GROWTH 88

CHAPTER SIX   FINANCIAL ABUNDANCE 97

CHAPTER SEVEN   BUSINESS ABUNDANCE 119

CHAPTER EIGHT   ABUNDANCE OF TIME 154

CHAPTER NINE   ABUNDANT GIVING 160

CHAPTER TEN   YOUR ABUNDANT FUTURE 177

INTRODUCTION

Abundance is a personal concept. One person may define it as having lots of money. Another may describe it as being spiritually fulfilled. A third might say that abundance means being healthy. What I think of as abundance could mean something totally different to you. That's why in this book I speak in a general way—you can insert your own personal definition.

Can you describe a time in your life when you felt abundance? Maybe you helped a stranger who was stranded on the side of the road. Perhaps you volunteered for a charity event. Maybe you were promoted at work and finally had enough money to buy that bigger house you always wanted. Or you simply got to spend more time with your family. Everyone has experienced random occasions of abundance. How would you like to be able to create predictable abundance in your life every day?

In this book, I will outline guidelines that I believe will achieve abundance on many levels such as financial, spiritual, in business, and in relationships. However, the foundation for all of these is emotional abundance.

Once you understand how emotions dictate every thought you have and every decision you make, you can learn the process of working through your personal icebergs, those negative words that continually loop through your head and prevent you from achieving what you want and deserve.

I believe that abundance is a constantly evolving cycle. Let's say you achieve an abundance of time. Do you stop there? No. That is when you ask yourself *what else* would make you feel abundant or how can you share this new-found abundance. To me, abundance is having more than enough! It means letting go of the emotional bondage of the past. There's no one-size-fits-all formula and no magic pill to achieving abundance. One must do the work.

To realize true abundance, you have to learn how to live intentionally and fight for yourself and believe in what you want. Nothing happens when you sit on the couch and make wishes. You must take action to achieve your goals. Inaction equals fear—fear of making mistakes, even fear of success.

Everything Is Perfect

So where does one start? My personal motto is *"Everything is perfect."* I believe that every disappointment gives me the opportunity to learn and to do better next time. For instance, I missed a flight coming home from China because I went to the wrong airport. It cost me $1000 to change my flight and rent a hotel room for the night. I could have been upset or even ashamed of myself. Instead I said, "Everything is perfect, and I am right where I am supposed to be." This has allowed me to be at peace instead of beating myself up and being mad all day.

Failing gives me—and you—the opportunity to become more enlightened. Before we go on, let me just say that I love sports metaphors. They really help illustrate both setback and success.

When I embrace something as a learning experience, it becomes empowering. If I embrace it as a failure or as a goal I didn't achieve, the next time an opportunity appears, I might keep the bat in the bag because I don't want to swing hard for fear of striking out again.

By sharing my personal experiences, I hope to show you what I have found to be the quickest way to eliminate the blocks that prevent you from achieving an abundance of love, joy, peace, kindness, and happiness. Once you understand how to create abundance, then you can change your frame of mind. Even more important, you can transform your life and the lives of others in a positive way. You already have the power within you. Now you are going to learn how to control that power to create an abundant mindset and an abundant life.

The most expensive thing you can own is a closed mind. As you read each chapter, try the theories on as you would a shirt in a dressing room. Walk around for a minute, and see how it feels. If you don't like it, that's okay. Hang it back on the rack and move on. But if you can keep an open mind and hold loosely to your current beliefs, I think you will gain the most from this book.

My Brief History

People ask me frequently how I figured out my path. Was it my parents' influence? Did I have a role model young in life that demonstrated skills and attributes to strive towards? The answer is no. My dad was a union electrician and my mom was an orthodontist assistant and had a home daycare. Middle-class would describe our family's lifestyle.

When I was 16 years old, I read the book *Rich Dad Poor Dad* by Robert Kiyosaki, and that message changed my life. In the book, the world trends towards the 'rat race', or more clearly making more, spending more, coming into more debt, etc. I decided that I did not want to join the 'rat race' but instead find avenues for financial freedom, including passive income that would allow me to follow other dreams and ambitions I desired.

I entered corporate America at 20 doing a job where I answered to others, had an earning ceiling, and no flexibility. There was a fork in the road presented to me when I was 25 where my employer told me to pick my path. That started my direction towards entrepreneurship. I have built a portfolio that now includes real estate (buy/sell and rentals), a manufacturing company, an oil and gas company, and a mortgage portfolio. I don't tell you this to boast, but I want to set the context of who I am before we get into how I got these companies.

The point becomes having a personal desire and taking calculated risks, rather than having a specific childhood upbringing, influencers, and formalized education in finding your purpose and success.

CHAPTER ONE
EMOTIONAL ABUNDANCE

Let's begin by looking at emotional abundance, or the confidence of knowing that you are loved, cared for, and understood. This is directly connected with the words we speak and hear. They have a profound effect on us, and how we interpret them affects us throughout our life. We've all faced negative comments and experiences, but unless we remove the block that tells us we can't or we're not good enough, we will always suffer emotional scarcity. We have to acknowledge how powerful words are. Remember words can do good and evil.

The mind is a powerful tool. It controls everything we do. Without emotional abundance, people often cause themselves unnecessary pain. A lack of emotional abundance in a job can result in a lack of integrity that can lead to lying, cheating, and stealing. In a relationship, it might result in staying in an abusive relationship.

A parent coming home from a stressful day at work tells her exuberant daughter who is singing to be quiet. "Stop that noise. You're giving me a headache," she says.

Even if that mother thought her daughter had a beautiful singing voice, she could have had a bad day at work and snapped at the child out of frustration. However, her words could translate in the daughter's mind to she isn't a good singer and has an ugly voice. That one statement might have destroyed the career of the world's next megastar.

Emotional Scarcity

Emotional scarcity comes from feeling that we do not have enough love, enough time, or enough care and understanding in our closest relationships—our parents, siblings, spouses, and children.

One of the first things I remember about understanding scarcity as a kid was when I asked my mom if I could order pizza for dinner, and she said we didn't have money for pizza that week. Although my mother and father were wonderful parents, that moment triggered my need to push away from scarcity. The scarcity was the feeling that not having enough money for pizza defined my worth. While this was 30 years ago, I can remember this moment so vividly. I can tell you what room we were in where my parents were sitting, where I was standing, everything. This memory is burned into my mind forever. I knew that I had to make the decision to live and act differently so I would get a different result. I told myself at that very young age if my children asked me if they could have pizza, I wanted to have enough money to buy it for them.

As I mentioned, my dad was a union electrician, and my mom worked as an orthodontic assistant until I was six. Then she started a daycare in our home so she could be with my two siblings and me. Sometimes my dad would get laid off, and I can remember times the church helped us out with food or money. That was when I began to set clear intentions that I wanted to be the one bringing the groceries or giving a check versus the one who was receiving the assistance.

My parents were very gracious. To this day, my mom will literally give you the shirt off her back. Even when we had little, she donated her time because that's all she had to give. She didn't have money, so she had to do the best with the resources she did have. Her example started me on my journey to discover how I could acquire enough time and money so that I would be able to serve others, help people in need, and be the person who was able to support himself and his family.

Most people do not understand why or how scarcity happens to them and that it's okay to feel emotions such as uncertainty and fear. One must acknowledge the emotion of fear or of feeling uncomfortable in a situation, and then let it go before you truly move into abundance. I was sitting next to a lady on an airplane, and I could tell she was obviously scared to fly. I started to talk to her and asked her about how her fear of flying started. She hesitated for a minute, and admitted that she really didn't know.

I said, "Is there a fear of crashing?"

"No not really."

"Are you willing to talk about it?" I asked.

She said, "Yeah, it is an interesting question."

"So let's take the worst-case scenario. What would be the worst that could happen if the plane crashed?"

She said, "I guess we could die or maybe worse we could live and have a terrible injure."

"Okay let's start with if we died. What is the worst that would happen?"

"My family would be sad, but I know I would go to Heaven," she responded.

"Okay, let's talk about if you got hurt. What would be the worst that could happen?"

"I guess I am paralyzed or a vegetable."

Then I said, "Okay, what if you were paralyzed or a vegetable? What is the worse that could happen?"

"Well, I guess my family would have to take care of me."

"Okay, so if your family had to take care of you, what is the worst that could happen?"

She replied, "I guess we would have less money because we wouldn't have two incomes."

"So what is the worst that would happen if you had only on income?" I asked.

"I guess we would downsize, but probably be okay."

After we started to address the fears she was having, we started going back up the ladder the other way with positive thoughts. I would ask her the same questions about if she were paralyzed or a vegetable what could be the best that could happen. All the way up until she said if she wasn't scared to fly, she could fly to see her friends and watch her daughter speak more. She loved those things and realized the joy she was keeping from herself for a very unlikely event. We tell ourselves these crazy stories that have a very low probability of happening and rob ourselves of so much joy.

Think deeply about a pain or fear going on in your life. Then you can arrive at a point where you can say, "Now I understand why I felt that way, and it's all right to feel that emotion. But I am going to choose to fight through the scarcity because I know the true gift is on the other side." Think of a baby before its born; they are very comfortable in the warm womb getting all their needs met. The day comes when they start to feel pressure. Fluids are flowing, and they are being forced down the birth canal. After the pain and being squeezed, they come out to a cold dry environment. What was a scary, uncomfortable, unknown situation is transformed into the gift of life as they enter the world. Instead of living in a confined womb, they get to experience sounds, smells, and an amazing journey ahead. Fear can inform you but not define you. Fear can awaken you but not cripple you.

One of my favorite books is *Fearless* by Max Lucado. In it, he says, "Imagine your life wholly untouched by angst. What if faith, not fear, was your default reaction to threats? If you could hover a fear magnet over your heart and extract every last shaving of dread, insecurity, or doubt, what would remain? Envision a day, just one day, where you could trust more and fear less."

What would you do in life if you had no fear? How would you live differently to achieve your wildest dreams?

Fear is a direct reflection of not feeling loved, cared for, understood, fearing loss and the unknown aspects of life. When one focuses on what they do not know or do not understand, emotional scarcity occupies the mind. From being too poor to buy pizza to being afraid of a plane ride, the story we are telling ourselves becomes that of scarcity and inadequacy, rather than abundance. Let's consider our limitations and what may sway us from abundance to scarcity.

Limitations? We All Have Them

Some of my friends know that I have dyslexia. Many who don't know me would say that someone with dyslexia should be the last person to write a book or even consider having that as an option. But my mentality is the same as Sir Richard Branson's of Virgin Records and Virgin everything else. *Screw it, just do it.* In my world, going against the grain makes life interesting.

Because of my dyslexia, I have spent my life going through side and back doors. In childhood, the other kids got to go through the typical path I call the front door; but I didn't learn the way they did, so I had to try and find another way to accomplish the same tasks. Growing up, I thought dyslexia was a huge hindrance and a curse.

The things that came easy for most students, even something as simple as reading aloud, were very difficult for me. While the other students read, I counted the people in the class to see what paragraph I would have to read so that I could practice before my turn. I did a little extra work while the others were reading in order to sound like I was a normal student. But the fact is I had read it 10 times before it was my turn.

In school, I was the class clown and would regularly get kicked out of class. My classmates thought I was funny. The fact was that

I did not understand the work, and if I was sent to detention, I could work alone and re-read the assignments until I understood them. Unfortunately, I was also disrespectful to my teachers in front of the other students, which caused even more trouble. I was so bad that another friend and I would have races to see who could get kicked out of class the fastest. I think most of my teachers would have bet that I would never amount to anything.

When I was a chef at a large hotel, my old school district had its Christmas party there. I had my full chef getup on with my hat and embroidered coat, running a custom-order pasta bar and entertaining guests while I cooked their order. Two different teachers came up to me.

"Justin, is that you?" one of them asked.

"Yes," I said.

"I thought you would be in jail or washing dishes somewhere," the teacher said.

At the time, I thought it was funny. But later, I realized just how bad I was...and how fortunate I was to get on the right path. However, once I understood dyslexia as I got older, I realized what a gift it was because it made me think differently than most people. In school, I had no options. If I wanted to do well, I had to work extra hard and make sacrifices in order to have the time I needed to learn. Most of the students could walk down the more traditional route and go through the front door. I had to find side doors and back doors because I didn't learn the same way they did. I even had to learn how to manipulate and even (while I hate to say this) sometimes cheat the system.

I was a good athlete. Although I played football, basketball, baseball, ran track, and wrestled, I loved football and was in the starting lineup on my high school team. At the time, I wondered whether or not I had a chance to become a professional and earn a lot of money. Even as a young man I was analytical, so I asked myself, "Am I good enough today to be in the NFL?" Knowing only the top .01% would make it to this level made me analyze my next course of action.

My answer was, "I don't think I was in the top .01% in the nation." So I chose not to play football the next year and began working and building a career to achieve my goals. Although I liked the camaraderie and fellowship, I knew that I could get those things outside of sports. I increased my hours at my job so I could start earning more money to create financial freedom in the future. Being willing to make sacrifices is also a part of the abundance mindset. You may think that your cup is full, but if you are not progressing, then sacrificing something will make space for a better idea, job, or relationship you desire to gain in your life.

Limitations become the rolling script that runs in our heads, which may lead to creating what I call an iceberg. The anatomy of an iceberg is that what is visible on the surface is only a fraction of what exists underneath the water.

Embrace Your Inner Iceberg

You will always run into walls. You can hit your head against them, climb over them, go around them, or blow them up. There are a hundred ways to get past a wall. Once you do, most of the time it is followed by another wall or obstacle. The tough issue is the pain and uncertainty you may have to experience before you break through. Embrace the iceberg of your past, and put it behind you so that you can move forward. What is the inner iceberg that is holding you back that you need to embrace to achieve your dreams?

Although I started to make this shift as a teenager, it doesn't matter where you are in your life, or what your story is. What matters is that you are intentional in your thoughts. You can start today, or you can hesitate because you think now is not a good time to begin to change.

As I mentioned, while my parents worked very hard, our family struggled at times when I was a child. I learned at a very young age that I did not want to grow up having those kinds of struggles in my life. I know some have had parents who could give them a head start in life, but I had to earn what I had through my own limited resources and hard work. From an early age, I felt the desire to go get what I wanted. In high school, I took early morning classes and left after lunch so that I could work basically full time. By the time I was sixteen, I was the youngest cook at a country club. I don't think I was any smarter than anyone else, and I certainly had a tough time learning. What I did have was the absolute belief in myself that I could do anything I set my mind to. In order to move forward, I had to embrace my iceberg of a learning disability and put the past behind me. I had to know that anything I wanted would have to be earned, not given to me.

Let me give you an example of a time when I made a choice to do something seemingly impossible. The very book you are reading I contemplated writing for only about twelve hours before I began on this journey. When I talked to a friend and told him I had a publisher and what I intended to do, he said that he had dreamed of writing a book for 28 years. He could have written a dozen books in that time. He even had the concepts and a list of titles, but he had an emotional block. Maybe it was because his family had always told him he had potential. He told me that being told he had potential throughout his childhood made him feel that he wasn't good enough now because he hadn't lived up to his potential.

Compliments can be taken in many ways. Something that was said as a compliment might not always be received as intended. Telling someone they have potential wouldn't hurt most, but for someone with a wound this might have a negative effect. Like the words to the little girl singing, words are very powerful. I talked to him about these concepts and urged him to start his journey because it is not too late. Ultimately, it is his choice. And yours. And mine.

Taking care of yourself and dealing with your struggles will make it easier to embrace your inner iceberg. If you don't take care

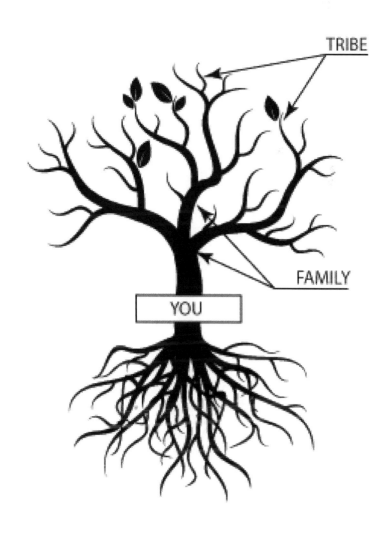

of yourself first, you cannot move forward to abundance. When your tank is empty, you cannot take care of anyone else.

This little tree diagram illustrates how taking care of yourself is the foundation for everything else in life. *You* come first. That's level one. You are the trunk of the tree. The branches closest to the trunk are your family. As you accumulate more, you grow more branches and you can begin to take care of your tribe, the people closest to you outside your family such as friends and members of your church. As your tree expands, you're able to contribute to your community, and then your country, and, ultimately, the world. Those who are able to care for others at a global level are the elite.

Although the Abundance Effect certainly includes monetary success, it is also a spiritual process. Taking care of both yourself and others means being willing to give your time, friendship, love, and help. This mindset covers the whole tree.

Imagine you are standing in the middle of the forest. Your vision would be only a few feet in dense timber. As you gain abundance, you climb the tree and see farther until you are at the top and can now see over all the trees with an unlimited wide-lens view. Sometimes, what is holding you back is that you are so close to your problem you can't see other solutions. You need to step back or climb the tree to get other perspectives.

Don't forget to take those comments and suggestions from others, and DO something with them. If you do not address those inner icebergs, you will continue to self-sabotage.

Intentions, Not Goals

I love this quote by CS Lewis: "Don't let your happiness depend on something you may lose." How often do we gage our happiness on things like money, houses, cars and success? When you look at most people's goals, they are typically a reflection of what they really value. Yet if we asked someone what they valued, they would probably say family, health, relationships, etc. Why don't the two line up in most people's lives? Perhaps it is the feeling of being pulled in contrasting directions between what you need to do and what you should do. To avoid this, I prefer to set *intentions* for what I want to achieve because I think that setting goals limits our options of what we think of as success, and that making commitments instead keeps me focused on the entire vision.

I don't want a good marriage, I want a thriving marriage. I want a thriving marriage today and until death do us part. I am committed to being the best father I can be to my children. I am committed to making a sustainable impact on the world. Focusing on these types of intentions instead of setting a goal to make a million dollars, or whatever you might want, will ultimately change what you value as important.

For example, what do we do when we cross the finish line of a race? We stop, don't we? I think goals are similar to this because when we achieve them, we either stop or we have to reset and make a new goal. I have found that holding our goals very loosely creates a more abundant life. The goal isn't the goal; the motion is the goal.

One of my mentors is Marshall Thurber, who is an attorney, real estate developer, businessman, educator, editor, scholar, inventor, negotiator, author, visionary, and public speaker. Thurber co-founded the Burklyn Business School in Vermont. It was designed to teach both the global principles of cooperation he learned from Dr. Buckminster Fuller and the contextual principles of the human potential movement. These had been demonstrated and proven in his own business. By utilizing Super Learning Technologies (for maximum memory attention), simulations, music and graphics, Thurber's teaching is known for being powerfully effective, fun, memorable, and leading edge.

Marshall's mission is to positively influence global convergence through consciousness and transformation. Marshall explained staying in motion through a process called *procession.* Imagine a bee. The bee's goal is to fly to the flowers and collect nectar so they can make honey for food. The procession is the pollen that gets all over the bee's legs, head, and wings. While the bee may think it is a nuisance, the true gift is the cross pollination of our planet when the bee flies from flower to flower. The bee staying in motion is what produces the gifts of all our botanicals. The gift typically happens at 90 degrees from the motion. Have you been so focused on goals that you had blinders on and missed out on some of the bigger gifts going on around you?

Now that I am more aware of procession, I literally see this in my life every day. Maybe it is something minor such as missing a flight and meeting a fascinating person. Perhaps it is something major like taking a small detour that results in meeting one of my best friends and business partners. I was in motion trying to achieve a goal when the procession happened and took me a totally different direction. At the time, I was going for something so small in comparison to the gift I was given in this friend and business partner. So where do you have to be to achieve a goal? You have to be somewhere else, right? I can't have a goal to sit in the chair I am writing this book in because I am already here. So staying in motion to achieve your intention is where the gifts are going to come from.

Even writing this book was procession. I was at a conference about buying and selling mortgages a good friend of mine runs. While I was there, one of the speakers talked about how writing a book had impacted his life. My intention had been to attend a conference to learn more about buying distressed mortgages. I left with the procession which wasn't even an idea the day before from one of the speakers, which was the idea of writing this book you are reading now.

I could have been in the back of the room checking emails and not paying attention. Then I would have missed the true gift I received from that conference. When we are too focused on our goals, we forget to be aware of the great things going on around us.

When you are in a scarcity mindset, your thoughts are skewed. So is your vision when you have a fear or problem on which you have a laser like focus. Your mind and energy are consumed by your fear. Conversely, when you are coming from abundance, your thinking is much clearer, allowing space and awareness for the procession. I can remember times when I was driven to close a deal because I needed the money. Those deals never closed on time and sometimes cancelled altogether. When I was in an abundant mindset, I always closed deals, always closed on time, even early. I am sure you can remember a time when you needed something so bad, and it didn't happen.

Setting intention is critical. You can hope for everything. You can say words such as *someday I want to,* instead of saying, *I am going to...* Those statements are totally different in intention and emotion. Say them aloud and notice how it feels because what you believe becomes your truth.

What You Believe Becomes Your Truth

Another book that has inspired me is *The Four Agreements,* by Don Miguel Ruiz. I will take a minute to share his Four Agreements because I think he is spot on.

1) *Be Impeccable with Your Word.* To me, this means integrity. Taking responsibility for all the words we say has the ability to set us free from some of our greatest bondage because words are so powerful. When we are kind and loving when we speak, we send out love. Most of the time, we receive it in return.

   I think of the mind as a fertile field. Words are the seeds we plant and that others plant in us. If we are being impeccable with our word, both in keeping it, and in how we speak to others, we have emotional abundance. We sow healthy seeds. We also protect ourselves from the negative words we hear. Those bad seeds fall on rocks and fail to grow within us.

2) *Don't Take Anything Personally.* I believe that when people make negative comments, that it's really a reflection of themselves. If someone speaks cruelly to you, it could be because they are uncomfortable with something in their life. For example, if someone says you are fat, they may be dealing with self-image issues, or if they say you are a liar, that may mean they have a problem with being honest.

3) *Don't Make Assumptions.* Don't assume that you understand the motivation behind a harsh comment. Assumptions can be poison. Gossip is nothing but assumption, and most of

the time, it is wrong. We can never know exactly what is going on in someone's life unless we talk to them. We typically make assumptions because we do not have the courage to ask clarifying questions. Don't assume others see the world the way you do or believe the way you believe. We have all had different life experiences that give us our set of beliefs.

Speak honestly and kindly. Ask questions so that you do not jump to conclusions. Bear in mind that you might not get an answer, but you will have made an honest attempt to understand the other person. Conversely, you should not be upset or put off if people ask you questions to get a deeper level of understanding.

4) *Always Do Your Best.* Although this one seems straightforward, it reminds us that doing our best fluctuates with the circumstances of our lives. This could be as simple as putting your laundry away neatly instead of just stuffing it in a corner. Or maybe trying your hardest at work instead of just showing up and going through the motions. When under emotional or physical stress, your best will be different from when you are at your peak performance. You may have more energy in the morning than in the evening, and you cannot do as much when you are sick as when you are well. The lesson is that when you do your best under every circumstance, you can stop judging yourself. When you do not do your best, you deny yourself your best self. Inaction is how you deny life because of fear. Living fully means taking action.

Emotional abundance is a powerful tool that will protect you from the most abusive person on the planet—you. What you believe to be true about yourself affects how much abuse you are willing to take from others. If you are operating from the scarcity

19

mindset, your belief system will tell you that you aren't worthy of respect or love or success. When you harshly judge yourself, you tolerate emotional, even physical abuse from others. If they abuse you less than you abuse yourself, you are more likely to stay in unhealthy relationships. Your belief system tells you that you deserve whatever happens and should be grateful that they are doing you a favor by being with you because you are not worthy of love and respect.

Humans are the only creatures that pay a thousand times for one mistake. When we begin to believe the lies in our heads and are ruled by fear, our mind becomes a religious hell, and we can make ourselves suffer for decades. Worse, our spouse and family may also repeatedly judge us for the same mistake.

When these types of injustices occur, our personal agreements become jealousy, fear, envy, anger, and hate. We are bonded by those and other scarcity agreements, both with ourselves and others. All of this stops us from living abundantly because we can't see all that God has in store for us.

You cannot achieve the state of abundance without recognizing how the past affects the decisions you make that lead to the effect a particular situation has upon your life. When you operate out of fear and anxiety, you block your ability to create financial, physical, and spiritual abundance. Nothing positive happens when your emotional tank is full of negativity. When you believe that you aren't good enough, you don't try. You can either be a victim or a warrior fighting for the best within you. The judge and the victim each fight to rule the mind and you must always be aware of what you choose as your truth.

To have an abundant mind, you must push through the negativity and fear. Once you do, you will begin to turn your life into what you want and deserve.

**When there are no enemy's within,
the enemy's outside cannot hurt you.**

~ African Proverb

Fear May Be an Illusion

Fear of the unknown prevents most people from ever getting started. Without taking some calculated risks, you will not succeed at your highest level. My experience is that fear gets fed with time, and the more time you spend delaying something or putting it off, the more the fear increases. Instead, try and address the fear as soon as possible. Let's say you are scared of making a call to someone about bad news. The longer you wait, the more fear will increase. Instead, make that call the first priority of the day when you have the most energy. The rest of your day will be better once you have that weight off your chest.

The first time I went skydiving, I began to get nervous as the plane started to climb to our jump altitude. I could feel the butterflies in my stomach expand in proportion to my growing anxiety about jumping out of the plane.

Twelve of us sat in two rows in a small but very loud turboprop plane. It didn't help my nerves that we climbed to jumping altitude within 10 minutes. It seemed as if we were going straight up.

Because it was my first time skydiving, I had to jump tandem. Now, I had a grown man strapped to my back who would control whether I lived or died within the next 20 minutes. My mom had grabbed the instructor and said, "I love him, and you better bring him down safely." Man, I love that lady.

I was the first one in line to jump out of this perfectly safe plane from 18,000 feet. Strapped together, the instructor and I waddled to the door because the ceiling was too low to stand up straight.

"Sit down in the doorway and stick your legs out of the plane," he instructed.

I did as he told me and felt the force of the wind hit my body. The power of our 150-mph speed only increased my fear.

"We're going to jump on the count of three," he said.

I nodded in agreement and gripped the chute straps on my chest and shoulders.

He counted, "One," and then lunged forward to push us out.

Not counting to three was a good idea, like ripping off a Band-Aid to get it over with quickly. Next thing I knew, the full force of the wind hit me like a truck as we began to plunge toward the ground at 130 miles per hour. All of a sudden, my fears were replaced by peace and the beauty I saw below.

Then the instructor tapped his altitude gauge and said, "Chute." He pointed to the ripcord and yelled, "Pull it." I reached for it as it flapped in the wind, gave it a firm tug, and we were hurled upward as the parachute expanded and filled with air.

Now we were just gliding and enjoying looking around. After a nice descent, we approached a bullseye, and it was time for me to try and land with a grown man on my back while still coming in pretty fast. We landed safely as I pulled my knees to my chest trying not to trip us. We made it, and, as I began to gain my bearings, I realized that I was shaking from the adrenaline rush.

Reflecting back on that journey, I can say that the time I was most afraid was riding in the plane to our jump altitude. Considering starting a new business or a new job is similar to putting the suit on before jumping out of an airplane. You start to prepare for the journey, and as you gain altitude, the fear of what you are about to do begins to paralyze you. Worry and doubt sets in as the unknown looms ahead. You start going through all the what-if scenarios you can dream up. You have choices. You can stay in the plane and just fly around or maybe go back to the ground and abort the plan. Or you can step on the ledge, take a leap of faith in yourself, and jump, expecting the chute to open.

If you stay in your comfort zone, you won't grow. Whether or not you fail along the way, taking some risks is the only way you can grow. Fear paralyzes some and empowers others to step into their greatness. Many people pressure themselves to avoid making mistakes. Never put that burden on yourself, for neither failure nor success ever completely define your life.

How Do You Operate?

Study the list below and get in touch with the emotions you feel. Think of a time when you experienced the scarcity traits. Now that you've done that, perhaps you can see that these emotions didn't serve you.

Scarcity Traits
- Poverty
- Sickness
- Blame
- Competition
- Desperation
- Hoarding
- Justification
- Mistrust
- Misery
- Shame
- Spiritual death
- War

23

Then study the abundance traits, and think of the times you've experienced them. When you're in that positive place, the outcome is far more rewarding and productive. Imagine how transformational your life would be if you operated from the abundance category.

Abundance Traits
- Health
- Wealth
- Confidence
- Collaboration
- Life
- Peace
- Prosperity
- Responsibility
- Sharing
- Trust
- Love

You *can* learn to analyze your feelings. When you feel shame, mistrust, or one of the other scarcity emotions, tell yourself it is okay to feel that way, but also that you must push through it because it is a scarcity mindset. The emotions you experience may be a necessary part of the journey towards changing your behaviors.

A friend of mine went through a very painful separation from her spouse, which took her focus off her business and created a huge scarcity mindset in her life. She went into hiding and did not answer her phone. I persisted in calling her, and when she finally took my call, I asked, "Have you brushed your teeth today?" What I meant was had she gotten out of bed, combed her hair, and make herself feel human? Sometimes people stay in this dark place, and doing some of the little things may help start them back on a path to recovery.

When someone is that emotionally devastated, it is very difficult to reach them. No matter how hard it is to listen to someone you care about who is hurting, you must send a message of hope and positivity. After I take one of these emotional charged calls, I take a short walk or break to replenish my emotional energy so that I can better prepare for whatever might happen next.

Another time, I had lunch with a woman who had been working for me for about six months. I had no agenda other than to catch up on a few items and to tell her that I appreciated her. She confided that only a month before I had hired her, she had contemplated committing suicide. She was deeply depressed because her husband had been put in prison. She had no money, no energy, and felt that she could not keep going.

She told me that her job with me had given her the opportunity to make great money, and that she was able to stabilize her emotions. Although her husband is still in prison, she has a new level of hope. She still has tough days, but now she is helping people in the prison system to get on their feet after their release. My hiring her gave her the second chance she needed. Both my emotional and financial abundance overflowed into her life. Now, her abundance is overflowing into the lives of people who are coming out of prison. For her, getting a job was a transitional moment to turn her circumstances around. For others, this may be finding an interest or purpose that drives change.

At lunch, she told me the story of a young man who was her husband's cellmate and guardian. "I feared that without the protection of this mountain of a man, my husband would not have survived at the time," she said. Her husband was a smaller man and his cell mate was a massive guy who let the other inmates know that no one was to bother him.

The cellmate is now on parole, and she is helping him get on his feet. She helped him find a job and even took him shopping for work clothes. While we were at lunch, she said he really needed a car so he could travel for his construction job and make better money. She was a little older and not that tech savvy, so she didn't really know how to look for vehicles aside from going to a dealership. She was so intimidated going to a dealership alone that she just didn't do anything about the situation. We sat in the booth at the restaurant, pulled up the internet, and found a used SUV for her to purchase for him. She called and made an appointment to surprise the cellmate with a used SUV so he could better his life.

It is amazing how you can save other people's lives just by being emotionally present and caring. You may not have a job to offer as I did, or money to spend on them as my staff member did, but you do have time to share and love to give as my parents did. I am glad I took the time to slow down in life so I could hear this amazing story.

We have to look at every circumstance and ask ourselves how we can use that experience to bless someone else. When I take the *focus* off myself, I also take the *pressure* off myself. This act allows me to turn the negative energy into a positive energy. Take your pain and turn it into power.

The Abundance Cycle

Abundance is flexible. You can change your focus anytime. You can add more options to choose among. The scarcity mindset will convince you that you can only work and go home—no other option. Or maybe you have two options, but you think that you must choose between them because you cannot do both. That won't work either. Instead of thinking: *I can either be good at my job or a good parent*, think: *How can I be great at my job* **and** *be a great parent?* So many people live a life of either-or choices. I would encourage you to consider using the word AND. Why do you have to choose either-or, when sometimes you can strive for both?

The abundant mind does not set limits. It connects with the larger abundance that continues to flow like the ocean. You can take water out of the ocean with a thimble, you can take it out with a cup, you can take it out with a bucket or a truck. You can even hook up a pipeline, and you won't see the level drop because of the vast abundance of water. You can keep going back to that well because abundance is endless.

As you achieve a goal, you create space to move to the next level. Say you have focused on having more free time. You have concentrated on it and reorganized your day or your week and have fulfilled that abundance. In doing so, you have created a space for your next goal. Now, ask yourself: *What's next? Where do I need to feel more abundance in my life?*

With more time, maybe you want to focus on making more money to set aside for vacation or to buy a car. Maybe you use it to spend more time with your children. Perhaps you divide it between the two. More time with your children means making more memories and being able to further mentor them. You may also help one of their friends, or make friends with their teachers or other parents. Those connections can lead to other gifts.

Abundance looks for ways to create multiple options that you can move toward. At the moment, you might use your free time to go back to school. In the future, you might want to investigate ways to save more money. When you live in abundance, you are always free to do whatever feels right for you. When the abundance snowball starts rolling, it multiplies in ways you cannot begin to imagine.

Abundant Thoughts

Below is an exercise to practice analyzing abundant thoughts. Take a few minutes to consider these questions and jot down your ideas.

1. What are your three best abundance traits? How can you capitalize on them?

    _____

    _____

    _____

    _____

    _____

    _____

2. Write about a time when you emotionally beat yourself up.

    _____

    _____

    _____

    _____

    _____

3. How could you have transformed that scarcity trait into a more positive emotion?

    _____

_____

_____

_____

4. Is there an instance or action that you or someone else is beating you up about that you need to let go of?

_____

_____

_____

5. What would you do if you knew you couldn't fail?

_____

_____

_____

6. What actions can you take to start achieving that desire?

_____

_____

_____

We all have a story that may or may not be beneficial to us formulating intentions, goals, and direction. As these thoughts arise, develop mechanisms for tackling your icebergs, turbulent pasts, and limitations. Then use these mechanisms to begin building resilience by continuing to sway your thoughts and emotions from scarcity to abundance.

CHAPTER TWO
THE ABUNDANT MINDSET

As I said before, my personal motto is *"Everything is perfect."* Losing a deal, losing your job, or having any negative experience can be very tough. However, embracing the concept that everything is perfect is so empowering because you build confidence and the desire to keep swinging the bat. If you don't accept that everything is perfect, you are more likely to get caught in the scarcity emotions of fear, blame, and endlessly trying to analyze what went wrong. Then you can never be optimally productive. You must battle through each challenge if you want to achieve abundance.

Can you think of a time you beat yourself up when you could instead have remained open minded to the possibilities ahead?

Playing Above the Line

People who play below the line not only hurt others, but they hurt themselves. Some of the emotions I would consider to be below-the-line and a waste are:

Shame – You may feel you didn't do well at something you tried. Maybe you let someone down, and you regret your actions. *If only I had stepped up and helped her, she would still be here.*

Justification – Instead of saying, "Sorry I was late for the meeting," you say. "I got stuck in traffic waiting for a train to pass." Or, "I missed the conference call because my last meeting ran long."

Lay blame – This one is all about not taking responsibility for your actions. "If my assistant would have sent the document over then we wouldn't be in this situation."

All of these emotions or modes of operation have one thing in common—you are making yourself a victim. Acknowledge that they are a waste of time and energy and accomplish nothing. What if we lived our lives as if we were responsible for everything whether or not it was in our control?

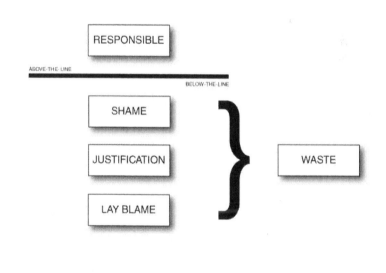

Playing above the line doesn't give anyone power except you. If you are late for a meeting because of a train, you apologize for being late and sit down for the meeting. Or if someone did something wrong, you move on and don't think about it again.

This is what I call being a Warrior. You take responsibility for whatever happens, good or bad, and move on. If we can move away from the below-the-line stances, then we can advance to the true gift of *everything is perfect.*

One of my best lessons in business was to learn to be responsible. That might be easy for you, but it was not for me. My problem is not being able to control all the variables, which makes me have to own other people's stuff as well as mine. I could be a victim and say how sad I am that someone did not choose to do business with me. I could feel shame that I was not good enough to do business with that person. Or I could justify what happened by blaming my failure on someone or something else. I know people who have spent their whole lives blaming their dead relatives instead of choosing to own their current situation and move on.

Think of a time when someone was late, they owned it and said, "I am sorry I was late," and then sat down. You don't need an excuse about what happened. Just take responsibility and move forward. Or when a team does not get something done, they try and blame the vendor instead of saying, "We should have followed up better or chosen a different vendor." It is that simple and so powerful, but I think few actually do this all day every day. Some of these victim traits have strong ties to childhood, but regardless of where the trait originated, being aware is the key to making changes.

Keep in mind that your best thoughts brought you to where you are today. This sounds so simple but is so profound. Think about this for a minute. We would never choose to make a bad decision unless we were trying to self-destruct. So that means that our greatest thinking has gotten us into the exact situations we are in or have been in. This concept was hard for me to own. In my mind, the situation changed, or other people had a hand in any negative results. The fact is, we do not take the time to seek wise counsel or the diversity of others. Maybe you did not do enough due diligence to see your potential blind spots or possible outcomes. Situations are always going to change, and when they do, you must make choices.

I met with a friend of mine who was going through a bad business breakup. She was involved in lawsuits and had hundreds of thousands of dollars at stake. As we talked, I thought about how her best thoughts got her into that situation and kept her in it much longer than she should have stayed. Now her best thoughts had to get her out of that position, and I wasn't sure they could. Most likely, she needed outside help in order to look at the problem more objectively.

How can you avoid these situations and constantly keep your finger on the pulse of the critical things you need to watch? I believe that most of the time it is as simple as listening to your gut feelings. Anyone who has ever managed a business will tell you that he or she has hired someone contrary to their gut feeling about the candidate—or regretted later not having terminated an employee they knew wasn't a good fit who ended up costing the company time, money, and potential opportunities.

Being negative is not the way to make progress. Have you been around someone who is always expecting the worst? How did that make you feel? The fact is, we have all been around that person and have probably been that person at some point. Being negative isn't going to get us what we want or solve any problems. It is just going to make matters worse.

I was watching *Naked and Afraid,* a TV series where a man and woman get dropped off with nothing but a couple basic tools like a machete and flint starter. They have no clothes and have to survive for 21 days together building shelter, finding food, and finding water in the middle of some pretty terrible places. This episode was in Africa, and the mosquitos were terrible at night. They were literally getting eaten alive with I'm guessing hundreds of bites each. They were in the exact same terrible place with the exact same set of circumstances. One chose to deal with the bites, as there wasn't much you could do about it. The other complained nonstop all day and all night about it. They both had approximately the same number of bites. One just chose to be mentally stronger and deal with the situation the best way possible. One didn't. In life, we have these decisions probably daily. Are we going to own our circumstances or let them own us?

One of my former employees always had a bad attitude in the office. At the time, my best thinking told me to leave her alone because she was good at what she did. As I look back on that situation, I see how her negative energy spread like a cancer through my organization. I should have been honest with myself, owned the situation, and made changes.

As the saying goes, be slow to hire and quick to fire. The cost is too great to hire, train, and try to manage just to let someone go a short time later. You are also performing a disservice to the employee, because he or she is probably not happy in the organization.

One of my favorite CEOs is Tony Hsieh of Zappos. In 2015, he gave his employees an ultimatum. In a company-wide email, he told them to embrace self-management by April 30, or they would be given a three-month severance package to leave. By May, 210 Zappos employees, or 14% of the company, had taken the offer to leave with three-month' severance pay.

Hsieh had encouraged people to quit and provided a financial incentive to allow those who were not going to be all in to support the company objective of a no-people-managers workforce. The people who left are most likely not going to be the ones who have a burning passion to help propel the company forward. On the contrary, they are likely to be dead weight that only slows everyone else down in their quest for greatness.

This is a very powerful message. Employees who are just punching the clock and only doing a fair job cost the company money. Most of these employees are probably playing below the line in shame, blame, and justifying. Employees like that will probably not be a catalyst for difference. They also have a negative effect on the culture of a business. So do not be afraid of weeding out the staff. Instead, get them out as quickly as possible. Long-term, you and your business will save time, effort, and money. Sound thinking like this got Zappos acquired by Amazon for a recorded $850 million.

Mindsets Affect Our Emotions

There are two types of mindsets you can experience. One is a fixed mindset that will take you nowhere because you think you know everything and you don't need help. In a fixed mindset, people believe their basic qualities, such as their intelligence or talent, are simply fixed traits. They spend their time documenting their intelligence or talent instead of developing them. They also believe that talent alone creates success—without effort. They're wrong.

A growth mindset will make you seek answers and force you to grow and learn. Within growth mindset, there are two subsets: linear thinking and exponential thinking. In a growth mindset, people believe that their most basic abilities can be developed through dedication and hard work—brains and talent are just the starting point. This view creates a love of learning and a resilience that is essential for great accomplishment. Virtually all great people have had these qualities.

One of my tenants called to tell me that he was going to be late on rent again. I asked what was going on, and he explained that he was working at a convenience store and wasn't even making enough money to support his family. I stopped him when he got into the story and said, "So what are you going to do about that?"

He said he didn't know because he didn't think he could get another job.

I agreed and said, "With that attitude, you are correct and shouldn't bother looking because you will not find one."

"What is that supposed to mean?" he demanded.

"That your mind is already made up that you aren't going to be happy so just go back to work tomorrow and deal with the people you don't like for the money you can't live on," I said.

Calling him out with some tough love got his attention. We talked for a while, and I mailed him a couple of books to help him with his self-concept so he could see how he was holding himself back from any type of growth and was creating a cycle that he had been in for years. I challenged him to look for jobs that paid more because he was worth it and that he would get a good job if he put himself out there and actually believed he was going to get something.

He called me three weeks later and said, "Thank you for talking some sense into me. I needed to hear that."

"That's all fine and good," I said, "but what are you doing about it?"

He said that he found a job making $4 more per hour and was grateful for my counsel. To some, this might not be a lot of money, but $8,000 per year to this family was literally a game changer.

That's how it works. Whether positive or negative, anything you focus on expands. You have a choice to be a victim or a warrior who can fight for what's best for you and for others.

The Past That Holds You Prisoner

A friend of mine is trying to break free from the fixed mindset her father gave her. Her father was from Africa and was raised very strict. This passed down to her, as he was very critical of everything she and her sisters did. She always got great grades, but they were never good enough. She was one of the best high school athletes with a number of full-ride scholarships to top schools, but all her father could tell her was she could have hit that pitch or she missed a play. She wanted to be a teacher, and her father thought that was a waste of time, that she should be a doctor. After college, she finally realized how toxic he was in her life, and she had to quit talking to him so she could start to heal. The problem was the damage was .already done, and she had a long road of healing ahead.

Being a new teacher in Southern California basically pays you a starvation wage. She had to have roommates and never had any extra because she was struggling to pay her own bills. She transitioned and started to work for a nonprofit, which payed her even less (which I didn't think was possible.) Her father had told her she wasn't enough, and she had started to believe it and was just getting by.

She has had severe anxiety and had to go on medication. Furthermore, her claustrophobia was so crippling that she couldn't get on an airplane. On one flight she was able to board while medicated, she had such a bad panic attack that the flight had to be diverted and landed at another airport. She has also suffered from a number of health ailments that maybe are a byproduct of the stress in her life. She had such bad anxiety that she would even stay home from work. The emotional wounds were so deep that she couldn't live her life.

I was out to dinner with her after she had landed a new great job. My wife, Lindsay, and I were congratulating her, and she basically said she didn't deserve the job and wasn't qualified enough for it. Now this is after probably seven years of seeing a professional counselor. Her father's voice is still telling her she isn't good enough. I am trying to help her break this fixed mindset of not being good enough to a mindset of more than enough and knowing she can do even more. The fixed mindset, possibly based on one person's opinion, has set limits on what she believes she is. I kid with her that she is an eagle walking around on the ground like a turkey not realizing her full potential. When she realizes her power and starts to soar like an eagle, she will be able to experience how powerful she really is!

Over the last years, she has been overcoming and facing many of her fears. We talked last week about how she has been able to overcome some of the obstacles. She said the biggest thing is getting some distance from her father. She had to make a tough choice to cut her father out of her life and have no communication with him. She said his voice was playing over and over in her head telling her she wasn't good enough. As silly as it sounds, she didn't like depression and had to make a choice. She had to make a conscious decision to not allow that abuse to be a part of her life anymore. One of the major steps she took was accepting she had a problem, like many other addictions. She needed help and couldn't do it on her own. She needed others to come alongside her and build her up until she had the strength to do it by herself. My wife and I were fortunate to be part of this support group in helping to build her up and encourage her during this dark time of her life.

She also had to seek professional help from a therapist and start on some medication to control her depression and anxiety. She made a choice to face her fears and deal with them head on. She still gets sweaty palms and feels her heart rate increase when she starts to get anxious. Before, she would focus on that until it got so bad she would have to leave work and go home. Now she acknowledges what is going on and just goes for a quick walk or stops and meditates. By doing this, she is in control and can fight off the demons. She has found a new power inside of her to allow her to achieve all the greatness we all could see in her before.

She has come a long way both personally and professionally. Two years after the flight diverted because of her panic attack, she was able to take on international travel flying 26 hours to India for a business trip without any issues. While she still had a fear of flying, she had to make a choice to face her fears. She went from a scarcity life of not having any extra money to lending money to friends to get better interest because she now has a surplus of funds. I am so proud of the growth she has had. It has been fun to watch her transition from scarcity to abundance in the last couple years.

Legends with Resilience

In 1978, sophomore Michael Jordan tried out for the varsity basketball team at Laney High School. When the list was posted, Jordan's name wasn't on it. Instead, he was asked to play on the junior varsity team. Jordan was heartbroken and ready to give up the sport altogether until his mother convinced him otherwise.

After picking himself up off the floor, Jordan did what champions do. He let his failure and disappointment drive him to be better. He played on the junior varsity team, and he worked himself to the limit. "Whenever I was working out and got tired and figured I ought to stop, I'd close my eyes and see that list in the locker room without my name on it, and that usually got me going again." He had a desire to succeed and worked harder than anyone in sports history. A couple of good quotes from Jordan proving he has a growth mindset are these.

> **I can accept failure. Everyone fails at something. But I can't accept not trying.**

> **I've missed more than 9,000 shots in my career. I've lost almost 300 games. Twenty-six times, I've been trusted to take the game winning shot and missed. I've failed over and over and over again in my life. And that is why I succeed.**

Mia Ham, gold medal soccer icon, played soccer at a young age with the boys a year older than she so she could challenge herself. When Mia was asked what the most important attribute a player must have was, without hesitation she said, "Mental toughness." When eleven players are trying to knock you down, and refs are trying to take your victory, don't you have to push through? When asked if she was the best in the sport, she said, "I don't think so." She had a will to learn even if she didn't think she was the best.

In a growth mindset, people believe that their most basic abilities can be developed through dedication and hard work—brains and talent are just the starting point. This view creates a love of learning and a resilience that is essential for great accomplishment.

When babies are trying to walk, we encourage them. We don't laugh at them when they fall down. At a young age, kids don't consider not trying to walk again after they fall hundreds of times. They get up and try again until they figure it out. Only do older people quit trying instead of pushing through to success. This is the growth mindset of trying and learning as you go until you succeed. New neurological connections are made by trying and pushing yourself.

Keeping Up with the Joneses

Today's social media makes it easy to see what your friends and acquaintances do. Your friends are building a house. Your coworker posts a photo on Facebook partying with his buddies in Hawaii. A neighbor buys a new boat.

When I hear or see people enjoying life or being able to afford a new toy, I congratulate them. That's great about the boat or the vacation or the new home. Not everyone is in that mindset. Instead of thinking abundantly in a personal way, they live vicariously through others.

You must remember that not everyone experiences an abundant life. Someone may see their friends on Facebook and feel left out. While Jim and Mike are partying in Hawaii, they may sit at home and think: *Here I sit on the couch for the third Friday night in a row. Why wasn't I invited?* Maybe they are having a tough financial year. They are looking at the pictures of their sister or their cousin on a trip with their families at Disney World. Instead of being happy for their relatives or friends who can take the trip, they become envious or jealous or depressed. Instead of planning how to earn their own vacation or new car or toy, they sit on the couch and feel like a failure.

Or they get caught in the rat race of keeping up with the Joneses. You get a raise and instead of saving or investing, you buy a new toy with that extra money. Then, you get a promotion and a bigger raise so you buy a bigger house to keep up with the neighbors. Before you know it, you have become what I call a Master-Card Millionaire. You take expensive vacations and have all the toys in the world, but you own almost nothing because you are making monthly payments on your lifestyle.

Who are you seeking approval from and why? What if you made a conscious decision to not care what others think, especially the one person you hold at the highest level? We all know that we are going to get knocked down. We need to know how we are going to handle it. If we give others the power to keep us down, we will surely lose the fight.

I have always made it a habit to live below my means and invest more than I spend. I am not saying you shouldn't have fun in life, but you also should not spend money you do not have. Waiting to buy the car or toy could mean the difference between the launching point to financial independence and living hand-to-mouth and just getting by.

If I want a toy, my goal will be to first buy an asset that generates enough money to cover the cost. For example, if I wanted a boat that cost $400 a month, I would need to buy a rental property or some other investment that would earn $400 a month in passive income. This would help me afford a nice luxury without taking the money out of my pocket each month.

I love this model so much that I wanted to help a young lady that babysits our kids live it out. She had been saving up her money for a while and was thinking about getting a newer car. I invited her mom to come travel with me to Detroit so she could see how I pick investment properties. I found two great investment homes for $5,000 each. I had the means to buy them and was prepared to buy them both. But instead I told this young lady's mom, "You should by these for your kids with the money they have been saving." The houses both needed about $2000 in work to get them up to a rental grade finish. The son had enough money to buy and the daughter was a little short so borrowed $2,000 from the mom to make the deal happen.

My babysitter went from maybe buying something like a not so good car or other depreciating assets to buying an asset that could provide her income. Those houses rent for $650 a month so they will have a stream of income coming in now for the rest of their life if they choose. She can now buy a really nice car instead of a used, okay car because the house will be paying the payment on it.

I encouraged the Mom to let the two kids deal directly with the property manager that I introduced them to. This will give them so much knowledge of how rentals work while still being able to come to the mom and I for help. My hope is that this gives them both a growth mindset and they start looking at finances differently. Helping a 17 and 19-year-old buy their first home hopefully can impact the trajectory of their life! When I see them, they are ecstatic and want to tell me what is going on with tenants or a repair they did. I know for sure their friends their age aren't buying houses and are looking up to them. It makes my heart smile knowing they get a passive income check in the mail that most adults don't even experience.

I don't want to go on a tangent about how to invest, so I will just speak about high level concepts. Before you jump into this type of passive income earnings, you will need to investigate what the interest rate will be on your purchases. Sometimes there is such cheap money available at 4% or 4.5% that I can make an investment and earn 8% to 15% by investing my cash and using the bank's money. If you cannot find a good investment, you can just pay the money you would spend on the toy to yourself until you have enough to buy it with cash.

I have a friend that was working on paying off a 3% interest student loan. When I heard that, I told her she was crazy if she paid that off early. That is some of the cheapest money available. Think of it this way: with inflation, will it be easier or harder to pay back money in the future? I say easier. If I buy $100 worth of groceries today I will get more groceries today than if I buy $100 of groceries in five years. So if you owe $10,000 today it will be easier to pay back in the future as money inflates.

It is profound how this compounds over time. So now I have the boat being funded by a property that is bringing in income. My taxes are further reduced because I am paying interest and getting depreciation, and, hopefully, the property will appreciate over time, compounding my gain.

Once I became aware that this could be done, I began to look at things differently. I find myself asking if an item such as a car is worth $100,000. It may only cost $30,000 today, but even at a modest interest, it will be at least three times that cost with the time value of money.

When you start viewing things through these glasses, it will affect your habits. Would you spend $15 on a cup of coffee at Starbucks? My answer is no, so I don't buy coffee from Starbucks today even though the cost of their coffee averages about $4 a cup.

Having a personally abundant mindset eliminates the need to compete with your friends and relatives who are either financially better off than you or are MasterCard Millionaires.

An abundant mind also looks toward the future and does not set boundaries. While people like to believe they will be making more in the future, it is good to be disciplined with your money. I like Dave Ramsey's quote, "If you will make the sacrifices now that most people aren't willing to make, later on you will be able to live as those folks will never be able to live." I know too many people trying to retire with little or no money because they weren't disciplined early in life. Now they find themselves working late into their 70s or retired and just getting by. They dreamed of travel and nice things; instead, they are trying to survive on spam and ramen noodles.

Disregard the Impossible

One of the most inspiring people I know is Nick Vujcic. I had the honor of spending time with Nick, and he is an amazing example of someone who has a remarkable growth mindset and total disregard for the impossible to achieve a successful life. I was fortunate to meet him and spend some time with him to hear a bit of his story. He is an inspiration on so many levels.

Nick was born without arms and legs. Yet, he is a motivational speaker who travels extensively, a husband, and a father. He swims. He drives a boat. He hits golf balls. In fact, Nick's motto is, "*No Arms. No Legs. No Worries!*" If you haven't heard of him or watched any of his inspirational videos on YouTube, I highly recommend that you do so.

Most of the leaders in innovation have abundant mindsets for sure. Larry Page, one of the founders of Google, believes in thinking big. He and his partners promote developing a healthy disregard for the impossible. Larry's two favorite questions are, *"Why not?"* and *"Why not bigger?"* This is an abundant mindset.

Look at the Richard Bransons and Donald Trumps of the world. Hugely successful people always say that you should never give up. Keep learning. Keep trying. They understand that the motion is the real prize.

I embraced the idea of never giving up and battling my way to the top. Actually, in some instances, being stubborn prevented me from reaching greater success. In his book, *The Dip,* Seth Godin says, "The old saying is wrong—winners do quit, and quitters do win." After reading the book, I did some research on Trump and discovered that he doesn't always practice what he preaches. Trump says winners never quit. If you look deeper into his past you will see that he has had many very expensive failures.

Yes, he has had many successes and has a net worth of around $4 billion. If money is your score card, he is a definite winner. He also has had many huge failures. Trump Airlines, Trump Vodka, Trump Mortgage, and Trump Casinos all failed. He filed for bankruptcy four times, something most people would consider a failure. He's also had several failed marriages.

However, one thing I admire about Trump is his willingness to keep trying when he knows that failure might be on the horizon. You would think someone with this many failures might be crying at home and possibly considering suicide, but the guy keeps fighting and, against all odds, won the Presidency. Media and the majority of the public said he couldn't win but he kept on fighting and found a way.

Sir Richard Branson, a fellow dyslexic, is another entrepreneur who does not think in terms of impossible. He has started more than 500 businesses and has closed over 200 of them. This is hard for me to get my head around because just starting 200 businesses is daunting, let alone closing that many. In spite of closing them, Branson's fortune is close to $5 billion.

Four years after a failed attempt to cross the Atlantic, Branson was the first person to successfully navigate a hot-air balloon across the Pacific. Although this adventure almost ended in disaster as he missed his destination of Los Angeles by 4,000 miles and ended up in the Canadian Artic, Sir Richard and his team landed safely and managed to set new world records for distance and duration.

His entire career has been based upon taking risks. At sixteen, he dropped out of high school and started his first business venture, *Student* magazine. At eighteen, he created the Virgin brand, named because of his and his employees' inexperience, and started Virgin Records. Twenty years later in 1992, he sold it for a billion dollars. Today, the Virgin group includes Virgin Mobile, Virgin Air, Virgin Trains, and even Virgin Galactic, which is helping to support space tourism.

In 2007, Sir Richard helped to form a group called the Elders with Nelson Mandela, Desmond Tutu, Kofi Annan, and Jimmy Carter. Their goal is to find new ways to end human suffering and create peaceful resolutions in difficult conflicts.

Thinking *why not* and *why not bigger* instead of *impossible* can help you achieve those dreams. This goes to show you that stepping up and swinging the bat is one of the greatest keys to success, in my mind. You might strike out sometimes, but if you never swing the bat, you will never get on base, let alone hit a home run. I believe that a little bit of fear is an indicator that you are moving in the right direction for growth. If you don't have fear, you aren't pushing yourself to grow because you are comfortable.

One of the reasons that Japan is not innovating, only copying, is cultural. Failure is such a disgrace to the family in Asia that people are scared to death to try something new and fail. The United

States is always innovating and trying new technology. Compare Japan, where failure is a disgrace, to the hub of innovation in Silicon Valley. Their model is fail early, fail often, and fail forward. I think the last part is the key. You have to fail forward. Failing isn't exciting but I think it's okay. You just need to learn from your mistakes so you don't do the same thing again. In hindsight, some of my greatest losses were also some of my greatest learning experiences that I now would not change for the world. Thomas Edison says, "I failed my way to success."

Transform from Wishing to Doing

Maybe you want to lose weight but spend more time on the couch than at the gym. Or you would like to spend more time with your family but golf three times a week. To eliminate the obstacles standing in your way, you must first acknowledge them. By being aware that you create most of your own roadblocks, you're more likely to succeed.

A question I ask is, "What is missing that, if present, could transform this situation?" Take this question and relate it to a specific aspect of your life.

- What is missing that could transform a relationship?
- What is missing that could transform a business negotiation?
- List your top three intentions that you want to accomplish.
- List your top three bad habits that stop you from achieving your intentions.

Taking the time to ponder these types of questions, as well as gaining diversity by asking others, can help move your mindset from a 6 to a 10 on the success scale.

This sounds simple, but taking action can be a real challenge. One of my roadblocks was the email rabbit hole. I would read an email and reply. Then head down another trail to read and reply to the next message. I might have stopped to look up information to share in another email. I would repeat this process several times a day, which only interrupts my work. Consider different ideas regarding developing positive habits and action.

Deviations from Developing Positive Habits

To overcome this email rabbit hole challenge, I set my email accounts on my computer and my phone to update only every four hours. This action protects me from myself, and I typically only check emails twice during a business day. My clients know that I will respond within 24 hours, which is a reasonable amount of time.

Our habits determine our future. Newton's Law of Inertia states that an object at rest stays at rest and an object in motion stays in motion. Our positive or negative motion keeps us going in a positive or negative direction. That is why the rich get richer and the poor get poorer. We must continually assess and correct our negative habits before they become coded in our DNA.

A boat that veers even one degree off course will have a huge deviation from its destination. Apply that one degree to a flight from JFK to LAX and you might find yourself 150 miles over the Pacific Ocean. One degree off course could mean the difference between making it to an important meeting on time or using your seat as a flotation device.

Think of a sapling with shallow roots. In order to grow properly, it needs to be supported by stakes until the roots get deep enough to hold it upright. If you try to wait until the tree is huge and crooked, it will be nearly impossible to correct. Deeply-rooted negative habits can be extremely challenging to break. But on the other hand, deeply-rooted positive habits can be extremely hard to break also.

We call these *slow variables*. It is like smoking cigarettes. One cigarette today will not kill you, but smoking over time can certainly kill you. A rocket's first couple minutes of flight burns more fuel than the rest of the entire flight. Getting started in the right direction takes time and willpower, so you must make a conscious effort.

Wonder Widely

To develop an abundant mindset, you need to give yourself permission to think about all of the possibilities, even if they sound crazy. Doing so opens up all kinds of ideas. I encourage you to write down all your ideas, even the crazy ones. After you have let your mind wander, then gradually narrow your focus. Go back through the list you created, and eliminate some that don't seem like a good fit right now. Then as the stronger ideas rise to the top, start pushing toward some action items. Those action items will ultimately be what help you achieve your new intention you identify.

I love what some of the big thinkers like Richard Branson, Steve Jobs, or Elon Musk view as a win. If it isn't 10 times better (or as they call it 10X), then they don't want to waste their time. To some, this sounds scary because you are setting lofty intentions that might not be reached. Our whole lives, we have been taught to set achievable goals that we can reach. I think this is a fixed mindset.

Let's say you wanted to make $100,000 a year. You can set an intention to make $100,000 a year. Even if you come up short and only make $90,000, feel okay about it. What if you 10X'd your goal and said you wanted to make $1 million a year so you pushed yourself to the limits to achieve it? Even if you only hit 50% of your goal, that would be $500,000, which would crush your original goal of $100,000. If you set a low bar, you will set a low performance matrix. By setting a 10X intention, you will push yourself beyond even what you think is possible. Dreaming big is what will keep you inspired to wake up in the morning. Dreaming small will keep you lying in bed, wondering what you're going to do today.

When you stop wishing and start doing, you will hit walls. That is part of the process of change, but you have options. You can change your system and go through or around the wall, or you can let the wall stop you and sit and suffer. When you grow, pain is inevitable. Endless suffering is not. Forget the impossible, and open your mind to creating an abundant future. To do this, you may have to invite other people into your life to hold you accountable to change bad habits and produce growth. Being honest and vulnerable with your situation is a crucial aspect of allowing people to speak into your life.

If you aren't willing to do it for yourself, maybe do it for others if that motivates you. We had a competition in my real estate company where we divided the staff into teams that were accountable to each other for making sales calls. On their own, people did not push themselves to meet a goal. They would justify why they were not making calls with excuses such as not having enough time or that he or she did not need another sale. They played small. However, if they knew that their actions would affect their team, they would push themselves to do their best. They played big, not for themselves but because they didn't want to let others down. How can you adopt this theory to hold yourself accountable and have those around you support you?

Playing small is a disservice not only to you, but to the world as well. You might be okay by not taking a risk for yourself, but think about whom you may ultimately negatively affect by playing safe. If you do not push through, do you think you can have the abundance to make a positive impact on the lives of others?

Be Vulnerable

Vulnerability is okay to show. Some see it as a weakness, especially for men. Some of us think they have to act like we know everything so that others won't think we are weak. I believe it is okay to cry, and it is okay to say that you don't know something. I think our natural instinct is to help people when they are vulnerable and say they don't know.

Even if you don't know everything, and you are honest with people, my experience is they will be very gracious to you. A person in my real estate office was really struggling with getting her business going. She told me she didn't have confidence to go out and talk to people because she thought she was too new and didn't know enough to have educated conversations with potential clients and even other realtors.

I told her that she needed to be herself and just tell people she didn't know what she didn't know. My experience is if you tell people the truth, they are normally very gracious and understanding. I told her that when she wrote her first deal, she should tell the other agents, "This is my first deal, and I might need some help."

When people have told me this, I have gone above and beyond for them. Sure, a few will try and take advantage, but the majority want to help and mentor someone. After we had this conversation, she came back into my office a couple of days later and said, "This was so freeing not putting the weight of the world on my shoulders." She has come to me crying tears of joy a couple of times because she has gotten over this fear or block. Three weeks after we talked, she had her first two deals going. She had been trying the other way for six months without success. Just removing this one block allowed her to get into the right frame of mind to succeed. I have no doubt that now that she has a couple of wins and confidence, she will do great. Being authentic means being true to yourself and not trying to act or be anything you are not.

Get Your Mind Right

Remember that all of your change starts with your mind. Acknowledging our bad habits, denying impossibilities, and being vulnerable are keys to developing your true potential. When you transform your thoughts from scarcity to abundance, or having big goals, it will aid you in disregarding the impossible and turn from wishing to achieve your dreams.

CHAPTER THREE
RELATIONSHIP ABUNDANCE

People are not meant to be alone. Whether family, friends, colleagues, or casual acquaintances, humans need each other. Our spiritual nature is called to love and cherish each other. The need for human relationships is also in our DNA.

According to Dr. Pascal Vrticka, PhD, research scientist at the Max Planck Institute for Human Cognitive and Brain Sciences, Department of Social Neuroscience, in Leipzig, Germany, "We are, so to speak, biologically hardwired for interacting with others, and are thus said to be endowed with a social brain."

We all have egos and want to feel valued and be told we are doing a good job or that we are a good friend or spouse. However, in order to create an abundant relationship, we need to be able to value others as well.

Relationship with a Partner

I am blessed to be married to my high school sweetheart and truly experience abundant love! I have the best, supportive wife who allows me to be me as I allow her to be her. I believe one reason we have such a strong marriage is that we share the same faith foundation on which we build our life together. While my story includes my wife, a supportive and loving relationship for you may include a partner who you may not call your spouse. However, the ideas are the same.

Not only do we both appreciate each other, but we also tell each other on a regular basis. One simple way to do that is by saying thank you. When my wife thanks me for working hard to provide for our family, it makes a huge impact on my day. Or when I tell her I am so grateful because she is such a great mother to our children, she's thrilled. It could even be something as simple as thanking her for doing my laundry and putting it away. I think most spouses take these things for granted, but a little gratitude can make the task a little easier next time. We text each other throughout the week with simple messages that say we are thinking of each other.

None of this is elaborate, like bringing home flowers and making a big scene. What is important is the constant flow of grateful reminders that we love and appreciate each other. It is a pretty simple recipe which strengthens our love and also is a great example to our children so they see how much we love and respect each other.

Everything requires balance and teamwork. Visualize two people on a sailboat. They are both holding the lines, and as one person leans out, the other person has to counterbalance to help steady the boat. If both lean inward in unison, they stay balanced. If one or both lean too far out of the boat with anger, resentment, and mistrust, eventually you will fall in the water. If you can find ways to lean into the boat, your partner will either reciprocate or fall into the water alone.

In his book, *Love and Respect*, Dr. Emerson Eggerichs says, "Cracking the communication code between husband and wife involves understanding one thing: that unconditional respect is as powerful for him as unconditional love is for her. It's the secret to marriage that every couple seeks, and yet few couples ever find."

That's very true, but if we're honest, after respect men want sex. I know relationships where sex is used as a negotiation card, and this behavior creates tension. I believe couples with sexual tension are the couples who consistently fight and pick at each other. My wife and I have a wonderful physical relationship because we both lean into the boat. My wife is aware of my male needs and goes out of her way to keep my needs met.

I also make a conscious decision to show my wife affection aside from just physically. We hold hands while walking or driving in the car. This simple act keeps us deeply connected. I initiate this contact as frequently as possible because I know it makes my wife feel loved.

Even at bedtime, we are touching each other before we fall asleep. When I say touch, I do not mean as a prelude to sex. Many men neglect to touch their wives unless it is to initiate lovemaking, but I mean a hand on her leg, back, or even our feet touching. I am very hot blooded, so we do a small touch instead of spooning. I would be open to spooning, but the fact is, I would be sweating and it wouldn't be comfortable or romantic for either of us when we are dying of heat.

Recently, I was sitting in my home office, and my wife came in to sit on my lap. We have been together for eighteen years and have two young kids, along with all the excuses of being tired or not having time to spend on "us." Newlyweds are so in love they can't keep their hands off each other, but as we get older and settle into a familiar routine, couples often lose that passion. That's why my wife and I make a conscious effort to stay connected both emotionally and physically.

I have seen relationships go through periods of stress where physical contact is nonexistent. I believe that both spouses must show affection without the expectation of sex. Both must not use lovemaking as a negotiation or a punishment to gain control over the other. Both must keep leaning into the boat to keep love alive.

Many dangers threaten even the strongest relationships. Physical affairs have always been a temptation in relationships. In the world today, emotional affairs can be just as dangerous and toxic due to the ease of connecting with another person through the Internet and social media. My personal opinion is that emotional affairs can be far more destructive than physical ones. It is easier to cut off the physical aspect with someone, as it is typically about sex, not a relationship. However, when you have a deep emotional connection, it is hard to turn off that desire, as the other person is constantly in your thoughts. Obviously having outside emotional and physical relationships is very toxic.

Although the rekindling of relationships and friendships is beautiful, and it is a great gift of Facebook, there is also a level of playing with fire. Here is my grade school crush or my high school sweetheart or the person you lost your virginity to. Or you see a beautiful girl on a beach in Hawaii who has just posted that she is having a wonderful time on vacation.

What begins as an innocent connection or reconnection can easily spiral into an emotional bond that, I think, can be harder to break and cause more damage to your relationship than if you had the physical affair. Rekindling an old flame reignites the level of want and feeling.

Another, more subtle risk is when one of you spends more time talking or texting on the phone than paying attention to each other or your family. They jump when the cell jangles, when a text chirps, and check Facebook a dozen times a day. One unhealthy result of the instant communication of cell phone calls and texting is the new addiction, nomophobia, the irrational fear of being without your cell phone or being unable to use it (as when the battery is low or you are unable to get a signal). Instances of nomophobia are rising as are support groups and evolving therapy to combat it.

I believe that in some relationships, this need to be constantly connected by cellphone or online can act like a subtle affair because the spouse spends so much time on the phone or online that he or she neglects his or her family. Similar to an affair, this behavior exerts too much influence over the person and definitely weakens the emotional connection between the spouses. When you are not fully present with your spouse, they feel like whatever is on your phone is more important to you than they are. Even if you are just sitting on the couch watching TV together, be present.

Everyone has witnessed broken relationships among friends or family members where one partner leans away, and then the other leans farther away in the opposite direction. The result is a constant battle until they run out of rope and both fall out of the relationship boat, which results in separation, divorce, or in broken friendships.

My friend shared a story of a woman who had given her husband an ultimatum that his behavior had to change or she would file for divorce. Her husband owned a business, and, from her perspective, he was selfish as she felt he spent nearly all of his time either working or with his friends. At the time, they had two young children, and he was rarely home because he focused only on what he wanted, while she focused on their home and children.

When she related this story to one of my mentors, Marshall, he told her about the effect of water on cement. The cement is solid and unyielding. Water seems harmless. Over time, the water will seep into the porous cement until it eventually cracks it. Marshall compared love and support to the water. He encouraged her to live by this water on cement metaphor and challenged her to be the water in her marriage and support her husband no matter what he did.

She started to "lean into the boat" hoping it would start to create a need for him to lean in as well. One of the things she disliked the most was her husband's annual 10-day motorcycle trip with a group of his friends. Every year she questioned his motives for going and asked him to shorten the trip. Yet every year he ignored her concern and went for the whole time.

Last year, she used the water on cement technique and didn't say anything negative when he was preparing for the trip. She told him to have a great time, that she loved him, and that she would be there when he got home. She exhibited a total mind shift, and that was when his cement block of selfishness began to crack. He went on the trip, but within a few days, he told his friends that he wanted to go home, and he did. For the first time in 10 years, he left before the rest of his buddies.

She was amazed that he came back early. That was a pivotal point in their marriage. They still have their struggles, but that moment was a 180-degree turn in the relationship. He is living more for his family and less for his friends. Their relationship is getting stronger, and they both are leaning into the boat. They went from the brink of divorce to expecting their third child.

It is a powerful example of loving unconditionally without any expectation of trying to change someone. I believe trying to change people is a recipe for disaster. That's not to say that you should let anyone walk over you, but when someone gets off track, "leaning in to the boat" to save the relationship often helps open the other person's eyes to his or her "negative" behavior.

The water challenge extends into our families, friends, and colleagues. I believe that we are called to love and cherish the people around us. The real thinking behind water on cement is to not try to change people. Just be who you are. If they change, they change. Don't use force and effort, and don't spend your life worrying about other people's behavior. Be who you are and make your choices. Opt in or opt out.

Through every challenge or success, I have had my wife by my side. I do not know another woman who could put up with what I do, the madness, and the different businesses.

When we owned an insurance company that my wife ran, I would call her and say, "We bought a house at 123 Main Street today. Can you please put insurance on it?"

Most partners would have a serious conversation before making a home purchase. I think it would be safe to say most partners would want to see it and be able to put their two cents in. We never had a conversation about my buying a house as an investment. She would just laugh and reply, "Great. I will get the insurance. When do you need it active? See you for dinner." There's a long-standing joke among the women in my office that if any of their husbands called with the same story, they would be dead.

On the worst days, when deals went south, I'd say something like, "Honey, I just ran two new BMWs off a cliff. It is like we lost $100,000 today because I did not insure them," her response would be exactly the same.

"That's a bummer. What did you learn from that experience?" Then without a pause or anger, she would ask, "How was the rest of your day?" People who know my wife know this is a true story. I'm serious. Her tone and manner do not change. We may have a conversation later about what I learned and what I could do differently in the future to prevent another disaster. Most spouses would get the cold shoulder or have to sleep in the other room or be told that they are an idiot.

Obviously, without a reasonable track record of success, that conversation would be a lot harder to have. Or if I began to have major disasters on a weekly basis, I am sure she would definitely have a different reaction. We have such a high level of trust and belief in each other that we know it will all be perfect in the end. Relationships can be hard and require effort to keep them on solid ground. Ideally, you need to include other relationships to hold you accountable and see your blind spots.

Mentorships and Positive Influences

Surrounding ourselves with positive-minded people helps to influence our life. Be careful whom you choose. Be careful of how you pick your mentors and friends because each will have a profound effect on your career and your life. Most people do not take that as seriously as they probably should. I believe that we need to look at choosing the people we allow close to us with a great level of care because they can have such enormous influence on us. As the saying goes, you are the average of the five closest people with whom you surround yourself. Most talk about this in a monetary sense, but don't lose sight of the emotional and mental influence as well.

We need people who can see the good, the bad, and the ugly sides of us and tell us what we might not want to hear, but that we need to hear. We also need people who will stick by us through the bad times as well as the good ones.

A colleague of mine went through a very tough time. He was ultra-successful and a great businessman. Everyone was his friend. Everyone wanted to be around him. He was invited to every function, every charity event, and every party. Then he started to have financial difficulty and owed lots of people lots of money. Within a short time, all those friends drifted away. The 30 invitations he received to Christmas parties all of a sudden turned into two or three from the people who were truly his friends.

When you are on top, everyone loves you. But the people you need to surround yourself with on a permanent basis are the ones who will continue to support and stand by you when you are on the bottom of the mountain working your way up to the top. Think of it this way. If you were broken down on the side of the road in the middle of the night who could you call for help?

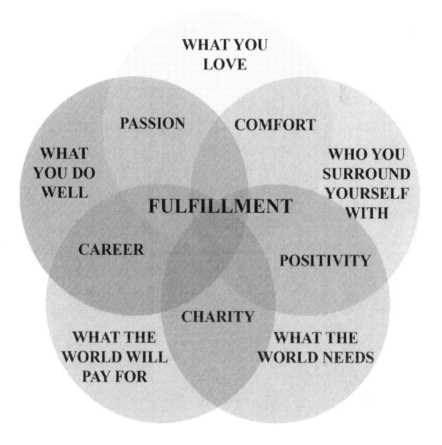

Your closest friends and mentors are going to have the most profound impact, so choose wisely. When I am choosing a mentor, I always like to see their score card in whatever I am seeking advice in. If I am asking someone for financial advice, I want to know that their financial score card is good. Not how much they are worth, but have they had a good track record of success? If I am asking someone about relationship advice, I think it is better to ask the couple that has been married for 30 years instead of the guy on his third marriage. One of the favorites in my industry is a realtor that rents and is telling people they need to buy investment properties. Never be scared to ask people about what they are doing to see if they might have sound advice or not. The people with success will be happy to show you, while the people that are fake will get very uncomfortable.

Then we have people that are colleagues or people that we have as friends, but maybe they are not best friends or in your close-friend circle. We may have spiritual friends who do not share the same beliefs, but are still people whom we admire and trust.

We also have friends we care about who may have different core values, and that can be hard to reconcile. Sometimes, we have to let those relationships go.

A good friend of mine and I owned a half dozen houses together at the time. When he decided to have an affair, his behavior didn't align with my core values, and ultimately, I could no longer be his friend. I still talked to him and explained why I did not agree with his decision. I told him I would still be his friend if he changed, but if he didn't I could not support his actions. Ultimately, he went ahead with the affair, ruined his marriage, and ruined our friendship.

Although our core values in business seemed to be the same and we both liked to help others, our personal values could not have been more different. Plus, someone who cheats in their closest relationships is probably at some point going to cheat in their business too. In my world, you cannot 'kind of' have integrity or 'kind of' have character. That should be true in your world as well.

One recommendation I would make when seeking a mentor is to look for one a couple of markets away from where you want to do business. When I was getting into selling foreclosure properties I looked outside of my market for people that could help me or that we could reciprocate by sending each other business. If I tried to do this with someone in my market, they would see me as a competitor and wouldn't share 100% of their ideas and contacts. By looking outside of my market, we could share openly, knowing that it wouldn't take business away from each other. While someone in your office might be helpful they probably are going to only share about 85% of the secret sauce. You need the other 15% that really makes the difference. Sometimes you will find someone with an abundant mentality that will share everything, but believe this is the exception not the norm.

People can cheat others and screw their business partners to get to the top, but sooner or later that house of cards will crumble. You may make it to the top without character, but you cannot stay on top without character. Be careful of who you allow to speak in your life, because it will have direct implications into the way you engage with others. It is important to hear everyone's input; however, incorporate only those that have weight and merit.

Be Present

In restaurants, people check their phones, text, even play games or search the Internet instead of enjoy the company of their companions. At home, every family member's attention is focused on anything but being present with the family. When I go home from the office, I do not check email, voicemail, or return texts or calls until my children are in bed. Even then, I might not check them unless it is an emergency. My wife and I have chosen to turn off the technology and be present with each other and our children.

Technology addiction is a growing problem. Sadly, this behavior negatively impacts both personal and professional relationships. I encourage you to spend face-to-face time with the people in your life and detach from technology. I was on a cruise a couple of months ago, and it was so refreshing for everyone to eat dinner and talk to each other. Everyone was present and engaged. The difference was that we were out at sea, and our phones didn't work so most didn't even carry them. We got back on land and went out to lunch with a group of friends. I looked up from my menu, and eight of the twelve people were back on their phones. I looked at my wife and said, "Wow. It was so nice when we didn't have technology."

Expect pushback when you begin. Every time someone asked why I didn't answer the after-work call, text, or email, I replied that I cherish time with my family, and that time is committed to them. When people know you are serious, they respect your decision. Occasionally, I must schedule a conference call during family time or there's a situation that I have to address after working hours, but that is a rare occurrence. This has become a joke among my friends that they have to call at five minutes to five, because I probably won't answer the phone after I finish work at five p.m. A friend of mine kids me that I turn into a pumpkin at 5:01 p.m.

Parenting Relationships

Technology-as-babysitter has helped to create a generation who are growing up with poor social skills. Kids tend to spend too much time on phones and tablets playing games or watching mindless videos. When you go to restaurants, you can constantly see parents sit down and give their kids their phone right away. Instead of the parent entertaining the child, they let technology raise them and speak into their life. I have two young kids and know giving them my phone would be easier but feel it is my duty to spend that time connecting with them.

Creating a strong bond with your children is just as important as creating one with your spouse. Although my daughters are four and six, at this writing, when I come home from work I ask them about their day and listen to their responses. Take time to engage, ask questions, listen intently, and give your children experiences.

We are teaching them to be confident and resourceful versus programming them to always have someone else make their decisions for them. Kids need to think and dream for themselves. If you are a parent, I recommend a book called *Parenting with Love and Logic*. It is a great book, and they even offer live classes. I think this is a great tool for empowering your children to be responsible. For example, my wife and I also empower them with age-appropriate choices:

"Do you want to wear your red coat or your blue one?"

"Would you like to walk to the car?" I'll ask. "Or shall I carry you?"

My favorite chapter in *Love and Logic* was when they talked about the Helicopter Parents. A helicopter parent is one that is constantly hovering over the child to instruct and tend to the child's every need. The parent, typically the mother, thinks that they have to be there and tell the kid what to do, answer every question for them, and get them ready. I remember friends that had parents like this. While my parents were teaching me to be self-reliant and fill out my own paperwork or make my own choices, my friend's parents were standing behind them telling them exactly what to do and when to do it.

The problem is that when the teenager leaves the house, they have been programed to listen for a voice to tell them what to do. Now their parent isn't there giving the instruction; it is another teenager telling them to smoke pot or maybe even have sex. They have been trained not to make decisions for themselves, so they may rely on others to make decisions for them. This is so dangerous, and we need to empower our kids to think for themselves. Challenge your young children to guide you through an airport. Let them start to figure stuff out for themselves.

My four-year-old and I were at the climbing wall at our neighborhood park. Although the wall is for children, it still is about eleven feet high at the top.

As she stood at the top, she looked down at me and said, "Daddy, can I jump off the top?"

All of the nearby parents and older kids looked at her as if asking, "She is really not going to jump, is she?" They also looked at me to see what I was going to do. I told her it was really high, but that I would let her jump off, and I would catch her. This was a risk for her and required a huge trust in me. She jumped, and I can still see her big eyes as she leaped away from the wall, peddling her arms trying to get her balance mid-flight. Luckily, I caught her, and we kept her fearless spirit alive.

It can be something as simple as touching a frog or a worm in the yard. I try to be a part of these adventures, as I know that my wife isn't excited about holding a snake or spider.

For example, we found a frog at our house. I was holding it so my kids could examine it, and then I put it in a bucket so that they could hold the bucket without squishing and squeezing the frog as kids can do. The frog jumped out of the bucket toward my wife, and she jumped back and screamed. We had to start the process over because the girls showed alarm because of my wife's reaction. She did not do anything intentionally. She has been programmed to be afraid. Kids watch our every move and they pick up on these small cues, so we must not let our fears be their fears.

We also do not want our daughters to grow up programmed to only play with Barbie and all that implies. We want them to be curious, independent, and adventurous. We want them to learn by experience instead of a lecture. I can either try to explain to my child what cold means, or I can put an ice cube in her hand so she can experience the feeling. As my fellow dyslexic Benjamin Franklin says, "Tell me, and I forget. Teach me, and I remember. Involve me, and I learn."

Every parent needs to empower their children with a growth mindset. To do that, you must be engaged with your kids face-to-face and not rely on technology to do your job as a parent.

Most children are born with a great capacity to learn, but parents and the educational system help to make them less gifted. Education systems teach at one speed to support all the kids. Say that your daughter is great at math, but in school she has to proceed at the pace of her class. Conversely, if she is a slow reader, the rest of the class may be pushing ahead leaving her behind.

As a parent, this can be frustrating. What you and I can do is take an active part in our child's education by filling in the gaps. Talk to teachers about a more challenging class for your math whiz. Find a tutor for your slow reader, or have her practice her reading under your guidance. It is crucial to help our children to develop their learning ability and establish a life-long love of learning at a young age. Sometimes it may mean enrolling your kids in a private school so they can learn at their own speed. I believe that spending a little more on education while they are young to develop their learning skills and habits is as important, if not more important, than saving every penny for college.

According to Dr. Benjamin Bloom, the professor of education and head of the University of Chicago's curricula committee, most children are born brilliant, but parents and the schools help to dumb them down. If I give a child a paperclip and ask, "What can you do with this?" I will get hundreds of creative answers. Maybe it is a gun, car, boat, or even a spaceship. If you ask an adult what it does, most will say that it holds papers together. As we get older, we tend to lose our creativity. I think as parents we need to spend time to build our children's creative muscles.

While doing my research, I came across a life-changing and controversial statistic I will share with you. The total IQ capacity of a human (how smart they are going to be) goes like this:

- From 1-4 years, 50% of the IQ capacity is established
- From 4-8 years, 30%
- From 8-13 years, 12%
- From 13-17 years, 8%

Ninety percent of our education dollars are spent after the age of eighteen, when we have little effect on the mind's capacity. We need to focus on the first 13 years and invest in our young children to give them the best possible chance to succeed. We wait to spend money until we send them to college, and IQ is basically already set at that point.

To be clear I am not saying that if you spend a lot of money during the early years that you will have an Einstein on your hands. I am saying that your child's IQ potential, whatever level that is, will be set. I would submit someone could have put Einstein in a box like our schools do, and he wouldn't have been as brilliant as he was. For you parents with young kids, two of the greatest factors of IQ development are experiences, which we talked about earlier, and your tone of voice. Yelling at a child has proven negative effects on their IQ, as well as other self-concept issues that are already known. Support them in whatever they are doing and tell them that you are proud of their performance.

Use Positive Reinforcement

Many kids deal with trying to make their parents proud, which is very sad. I went through this with my father. I knew he loved me because he showed that through his actions. But I could not recall one time growing up when he verbally said he loved me or that he was proud of me.

I participated in a Wild at Heart workshop based on John Eldredge's book. The workshop forced me to acknowledge that I had some unresolved father issues and took me through an exercise to unlock them. Our group consisted of about fourteen men, and all but one of us had had the same hurtful experience with their father not telling them they loved them.

One of the exercises was to try to peel back the layers of the onion that was your dad's life. As you do this, you may start to justify his actions, but that's not the intention. My father came from a broken family. His parents separated at a young age, and his mother had a number of husbands, none of whom were a good role model including one alcoholic. So he had been programmed from childhood not to tell his children that he loved them because no man told him that he was loved. After that, he left home and joined the Army. We all know that no one in the service wrapped their arms around him and told him that they were proud of him or that they loved him. In taking a step back from your emotions, you can see what caused your situation.

Although I still have some struggles, I am working on it. It is good to be aware of what made him emotionally closed. Like him, I was never much of a hugger or a person who told others I loved them. This was obviously a byproduct of how I was raised, and the code that was written on my heart. Since I became aware of why I operated that way, I made a vow to break the cycle. I hold and kiss and tell my daughters that I love them many times every day.

The stakes are even higher to show love for our daughters. When the father isn't engaged in the daughter's life, there are so many byproducts of the young woman searching for love in all the wrong places. They need someone to tell them that they are loved, or they may enter into unhealthy relationships. They may accept abuse because their mom accepted it. It is so crucial to be a good role model and a good example, especially for your daughters.

I do not know what your story may be, but I encourage you to do a few things if you are going through a similar struggle.

- Peel back the layers of the onion and ask yourself how was your dad raised? How was your grandfather raised? Maybe your mom was the tough one. Ask the same questions about her. This can provide you with some insight as to why he or she acted as they did.

- Let go of the past and understand that you have a choice as to how you treat others. Also, remember that forgiving is different from forgetting. Some very bad things have happened in people's lives, and I am not saying you will ever forget some of those moments. But I think there is something very freeing about forgiving someone for whatever it was. We hold this anger and tension inside us, and it is a poison eating us up. We drink the poison and expect it to affect the other person. Releasing them is really just getting that poison out of your body so you can truly heal. This breaks the cycle of anger being passed down to another generation.

- If you think it would be healing, have a conversation with the individual that hurt you. Be non-confrontational. You could mention that you read this book, and it brought up some interesting issues that you would like to talk about.

Five years ago, I used the Wild at Heart study to initiate this conversation with my father. I told him that I was going through a study, and it was very eye opening. I let him know that it hurt that he didn't tell me he loved me. He would tell a neighbor he ran into at the store how great I was, but he never told me. As a child, that was one of my drivers in sports and early in my career. I pushed myself so hard, hoping he would say, "Well done, Son," or "I am proud of you."

During that conversation, my father explained to me that he loved me very much and was very proud of me. I think the fact was he just wasn't aware because those were the glasses that he had been programmed to look through in his life. He wasn't aware of how that made me or my siblings feel. For him, it was just another day, but for us, it was the making of our story. Positive reinforcement may fill in the gap and change the stories we tell ourselves. As parents, we must be conscious of how we speak to our children to avoid the emptiness they may feel due to our lack of positive reinforcement.

Building New and Restoring Damaged Relationships

When you spend time with your family, your spouse, your colleagues and your friends, stay present in the moment. This is old advice, but, unfortunately, I think we are getting farther and farther away from actively listening and conversing with other people. That is why God gave us two ears to listen and one mouth to talk.

A powerful way to build a new relationship or restore a neglected one is to be more interested in them than you expect them to be interested in you. No one wants to sit and listen to someone do nothing but talk about themselves all night. Ask thoughtful questions. Do not only ask whether they have children. If they say yes, ask how many? Ask their names and ages. Are they boys or girls? What do they like to do? People love to talk about themselves, and if you continue to drill down, they will feel you are truly interested in them.

When you listen more and talk less, you receive the bonus of a better experience too. Imagine if you went on your first date and sat there talking about yourself the whole time without once asking your date about him or herself. The person would not be interested in a second date. If you are always competing with *me too* stories, you can cause stress. Me too stories are when someone tells you about their trip, but instead of being excited and acknowledging them you go into the story of when you were on vacation and did (fill in the blank). Of course you should share your experiences, but you do not want to be the person who continually tries to one-up everyone else.

Another way to build strong relationships is to keep the abundant mindset and continue to share. Personally, it is easier for me to be a giver instead of a receiver. I frequently get phone calls from people whom I do not know who came to me through my network and thought that I could help them and be a good resource. Helping others is very rewarding. I am working on being a better receiver, but it is still a struggle for me. Even when people try to buy me lunch, I try and fight them. I need to be better at just thanking them and shutting up.

For strained relationships, try to take an objective step back. I close my eyes, and imagine the person and the situation as if I were watching a TV program. As I visualize the interaction, I ask myself, "What are they feeling? What are they thinking?"

Three Questions to ask in a conflict are:
1. What assumptions am I making?
2. What is the other person thinking, feeling, and wanting?
3. How else can I think about this?

Someone who was working with me on an oil and gas deal seemed to not be doing his job properly. I did the exercise above and began to think that maybe he did not understand his job and was fearful of acting because he might make a mistake. I was right. Taking a few moments to imagine his perspective helped me to ask more thoughtful questions the next time we met. I discovered that he did not know what to do but was reluctant to ask for advice. I was able to offer him the help he needed, and he became a valuable member of our team.

This exercise is not always going to repair the problem. Maybe it validates that you need to remove yourself from an unhealthy situation, which will be a positive step for you.

Focusing on building new and strengthening damaged relationships may lead to having a more fulfilled personal life. Meeting new people and investing into others may improve and/or build your skill set in interactions and maintenance as those relationships improve.

Building Business Relationships

A friend of mine, Bill, says, "The road to success is paved with great inconveniences." If you want strong business relationships, you must go out of your way to create them. In 2008, when foreclosures were in full swing, I sold an average of 250 homes a year and was the top foreclosure agent in Northern Colorado. I had been recognized by the *Wall Street Journal* as one of the top 50 realtors from more than a million realtors nationwide.

At a time when other realtors emailed their contacts and sent cards to prospective clients, I flew across the country to cater lunches for the whole office staff and take key people out to dinner. This was very expensive and very inconvenient, but I knew building that relationship would be the way to grow my business. My intention going into those meetings was to make a new friend.

Of course, the people I visited knew that I would love their business, but they also knew that I would respect their decision.

Although they had not added a new agent for decades, I visited Fannie Mae for years. My intention was to establish a good relationship, so in the event they did have an opening, my name would be at the top of their list. I remember the day Fannie Mae, the largest holder of foreclosed homes in the US, called me and said that I had been approved to be in their network. Other clients began to respond in the same fashion. If they had five properties to list, three would come to me. These people wanted to work with someone they knew and considered a friend. Once we had the account, we obviously had to perform. Just being friends wouldn't justify nonperformance.

How could you go above and beyond to build new clients or further relationships with current clients? Honing in on those relationships and going out of your way to build them can result in huge growth. The bonus is that many of these contacts are still my friends. When they move to other companies and need help, they call me.

Another positive outcome of reaching out to as many people as possible is that you will stay ahead of the industry. Pivoting and watching where I thought the market was going to be in the next three years helped me achieve a high level of success. As Wayne Gretzky, a hall of fame hockey player, says, "Go to where the puck is going, not to where it has been."

Abundant Relationships

Below is an exercise to practice analyzing abundant relationships. Take a few minutes to consider these questions, and jot down your ideas.

1. Is there a relationship that needs healing?

_____

_____

2. What action steps can you take to lean into the boat?

_____

_____

_____

3. What action item can you commit to so you are a better parent or spouse/partner?

_____

_____

4. In what ways can you try to be more "interested" in others rather than "interesting"?

_____

_____

In conclusion, relationships matter, and it matters how you "show up" in each of those relationships. We have an opportunity to speak into people's lives and create either a positive or negative impact. Your quality of life should improve with meaningful and abundant relationships.

CHAPTER FOUR
ABUNDANT VISION

How big would your future be if you were not afraid to fail?

Think about that for a minute. Failure is usually an inevitable part of success. When you begin to develop a level of fearlessness and objectivity, you create an abundant vision of *there is and always will be enough.*

Fear of failure prevents many people from ever getting started. When you operate from a growth mindset that allows you to keep trying no matter what happens, you attract more opportunities. If one path does not work, you automatically try another. If one business model does not prosper, you take a different approach. If the product does not sell, you refine it or scrap it and begin again.

Passion Drives Vision, Pivoting Fuels Success

No matter what your vision, if you are not passionate about achieving it, you won't. It is easier to talk yourself out of something than to keep pushing forward through the struggles until you succeed.

Breaking your vision down into small, manageable steps helps to remove the fear. So does operating from a high-grade thinking pattern where you can step back and look objectively at your goals. How much time can you devote? Which opportunity will need the highest capital investment? Which one has the highest potential reward, such as financial gain or flexibility? Analyzing the process is another tool that may remove some of the anxiety. However, sooner or later you must take that leap of faith. An African proverb says, "When there are no enemy's within, the enemy's outside can do us no harm."

Analysis paralysis can stop you cold, too. Instead of doing something, you sit and digest the data, chew on the alternatives, and eventually talk yourself out of taking those first steps. Steve Jobs put it this way, "If you can't make your mind up, just make a decision." Any movement is better than staring into space as opportunity passes by. If you are looking at two hills, instead of sitting around trying to figure out which is best, just pick one and go. By the time you finally decide, you could have already climbed both.

PayPal began in 1998 as Confinity, a company that developed security software for hand-held devices such as Palm Pilot. When that service did not generate much interest, founders Max Levchin, Peter Thiel, Luke Nosek, Elon Musk, and Ken Howery pivoted and developed PayPal as a money transfer service. In 2000, they merged with x.com, an online banking service. In 2001, x.com was renamed PayPal and began a relationship with eBay. The market expanded so fast that by 2002, eBay bought PayPal for $1.5 billion. Today, PayPal has more than 159 million user accounts in 203 worldwide markets that generate approximately $8 billion in revenue. If the PayPal founders weren't willing to listen to the market, they would have closed the company. They were willing to put what they thought was a good idea of transferring money through Palm Pilots aside for an idea the market said they wanted, which was paying for items securely online. Pivoting and holding our ideas loosely can be very profitable. By holding onto an idea and being strong headed, you can miss a great opportunity to pivot.

Know Your Purpose

Purpose can change, but it never is complete. When I think of purpose, or what some call your *why*, I envision it as too big to achieve within one's lifetime.

Say that you want the world to have clean water. If you are having a growth mindset and setting lofty purpose, this is going to take a really long time to work out, so you will probably never cross the finish line. You will have lots of progress and will hopefully have a great impact on your purpose over time.

In both life and business, you need to love. It's not enough to *like;* you have to *love* what you are doing. Without passion, your work will drain you to the point of giving up. That is why you must understand the full scope of the job you want. Maybe you want to be a motivational speaker. Remember that actual speaking is probably 10% of the job. You may be focusing on the fun part and not considering the entire job requirement. You spend a great amount of time in hotels and away from your family, on airplanes, in taxis, studying, at seminars, and on conference calls. All of these logistical tasks must take place before you actually stand on stage to speak. Look at Oprah. She spends a full day on interviews, management, preparation, dressing, makeup, and hair styling, all for a one-hour show.

I am not trying to talk you out of doing something you love. I do encourage you to take the time to look at the full scope before you jump in with both feet. I know tech startup people who thought they were going to be the next Facebook and make billions with their ideas. However, they didn't look at the full scope of sleeping under their desk, working 80 hours a week, and eating nachos from 7/11. They only had the end game in mind versus the work and time needed to get to that level.

John Assaraf, a serial entrepreneur, brain researcher, and CEO of NeuroGym, says, "Am I willing to trade my life for the accomplishment of these goals?" Are you willing to miss dinner with your family? Trade money or time to achieve your goals? There will need to be sacrifices.

Set Priorities and Stick to Them

Keeping your vision in mind includes setting priorities and then not getting distracted. One of my favorite stories about Richard Branson's fierce determination not to be swayed comes from Darren Hardy. In his book, *The Entrepreneurial Rollercoaster*, Hardy says that he was once asked by a client to contact Sir Richard on their behalf and request that he speak at their annual conference. They offered him $100,000 for the one-hour keynote.

Branson's staff rejected the offer. The company increased their offer to $250,000, and was rejected again. They increased the offer to $500,000 and sweetened the deal with transportation on a private jet. That offer was rejected as well. Finally, in a desperate last move, the client told Hardy to ask Branson to name his price. His secretary responded that it wasn't about the money. Sir Richard Branson has a short list of three top priorities, and speaking for a fee is not one of them.

Of course, Richard Branson can afford to turn down $500,000 for an hour of speaking, but that is not the point. Unless you limit your priorities, you might as well have none, because you will scatter your energy trying to make everything a priority.

Maybe your priority is to take more vacations. Perhaps you want to save extra money for retirement. Maybe you want to have more time to develop your own business. Whatever your vision is, setting one, two, or three priorities to reach and then pursuing those priorities with the single-mindedness of Sir Richard, will help you to succeed.

I thought that he was really smart to prioritize, or as I call it high grade. What surprised me was hearing what he did with the rest of the list. He throws it away because it distracts from what is truly important. I think we can be good at setting priorities and bad at keeping them. I can only speak for myself when I say I set priorities then get caught up in other tasks or items that are not on my top three lists.

You may think that having a long list of priorities and jumping back and forth between them is multi-tasking, but you are really only doing multiple tasks at a slower pace. By multi-focusing on the top three, you work just as hard, but you get better results because you are not trading off on a task that you can push to the max.

Southwest Airlines co-founder Herb Kelleher says their purpose is "to connect people to what's important in their lives through friendly, reliable, and low-cost air travel". Because they are clear on their purpose, they view all things through those ideals. They don't offer first class seating; they don't serve meals because it doesn't help them achieve being the low-cost airline. They don't charge for bags because that would make customers travel more expensive. If someone suggested adding more leg room, they would have to ask, "Will doing this help us keep our fairs low?"

I read an interview from Kelleher about a woman that was complaining about no assigned seats, no first class, and waiting in a line like cattle. Kelleher wrote back simply, "I am sorry we will miss you." It was a great lesson to not apologize for what we believe. If this is how your company believes it can deliver the best product to consumers, realize you aren't going to please everyone and don't fight the ones that don't like it.

Decide on your main focus, and do not allow other outside pressures to persuade you away from your core values and priorities. Often times, it may be valuable to seek a second opinion to help reevaluate or confirm your vision.

Get a Second Opinion

One of my friends called me to look at a product he is trying to get to market. He had invented a breathing strip that did a much better job at opening the nasal septum than other strips on the market. However, he was so close to the project that he could not see the blind spots.

He was positioning the whole campaign towards how it could be used in sports and at the gym. He had created two videos showing people wearing his product while working out and participating in sports. He even had a famous football player that was endorsing the product.

I did a little research on the industry leader, Breathe Right strip, a competitive product. Ninety-five percent of their revenue is generated by people who use the product while sleeping, not athletics. My question to him was, "So if a company is making $100 million with this approach, why would you position your strip to fix something that people are not asking for help on?"

My thoughts were that he was targeting a market that does not exist. I have played sports all my life and never used a breathing strip. I also did not think that very many people would wear one while going for a run or at the gym. Helping to prevent snoring, as Breathe Right does, made sense.

When I told him my thoughts, he said that the pro athlete's wife had told him that the best part about the breathing strips was her husband quit snoring. Of course I asked why her comment wasn't used as a testimonial.

The point is, sometimes we get going down a path where we need to pivot, but we are too close to the product that we don't see these things. You need to ask people and give them permission to be totally honest with you. I call this Level-10 accountability. If the product sucks, please do not pull any punches—just call it like you see it without a filter.

Many people try to be too nice to their friends, which actually hurts them in the long run. Had I not shared candid advice with my friend because I did not want to hurt his feelings, and he had stayed on that course two more years hitting his head against the wall, I would have felt terrible. That said, if you give feedback and they do not use it, that is their choice. But I think we have to at least ask for permission to be honest, and then do just that.

This will help you pivot faster so you can fail forward. You do not have to agree with or even take someone's opinion. You should listen objectively. Their ideas and opinions could lead you to form another idea that will work better. Just be careful that you don't spend too much time getting advice, as that could halt production instead of taking some action.

Choose the Right Product and the Right Customer

A 2013 article on *Entrepreneur.com* presented three principles for achieving success.

1. **Work on a problem you are passionate about solving.** Only start a company if you are willing to spend 80 to 100 hours a week working on it without getting paid. When you get started, you will probably need to do this and convince others to do it as well. Without passion, you won't last.

2. **Build a prototype.** Think about your startup product and then build a quick and inexpensive version of it. Building such a prototype will help you communicate what you are trying to accomplish with potential customers.

   Finding that first customer—your foot in the door to targeting a market—depends on how people respond to your prototype.

3. **Find customer pain.** As much as you believe you will be the exception, most startups fail. That's why startups must focus on targeting customers with significant pain (needs) that competitors are not addressing. Then the startup must create a low-risk way to encourage customers to try the product.

Applying these principles will work in your personal life as well. Say that you want to take more of those vacations. Your pain, or need, is that you either do not have the time or the money or both. Working on the problem may consist of revising your budget so you can save a few dollars each month for a trip.

Tie Your Vision to a Dynamic Value

Dynamic Value, or DyVal as my mentor Marshall Thurber calls it, means that you create a business or product that has a greater value than the cost; one that sets you and your product apart from the rest of the market

The American Girl doll includes different cultures and races and offers books that touch on sensitive subjects such as slavery, animal abuse, and child abuse. Each doll has a different combination of face mold, skin tone, eye color, and hair color, length, texture, and/or style. American Girl states that this variety allows customers to choose dolls that "represent the individuality and diversity of today's American girls." Compare that experience with Mattel's Barbie. While Barbie dolls start at around $20, an American Girl costs $95 for a doll and book. American Girl's DyVal is on creating an experience rather than simply a doll.

Apple store sales-per-square-foot is one of the highest in the world because they have created a positive customer experience in a culture with very loyal following. Each Apple store staff has extensive training on how to create an environment where the customer feels as if he or she is the only one in the store. In a very competitive industry, Apple also sets itself apart with a product that is extremely user-friendly. That and their approach to customer service have paid off.

In 2014, Apple did about $182 billion in revenue with $35 billion in profit, more than double of all the other computer companies combined. This proves that you can create a better customer experience in every market, even the most competitive ones. What other company has customers camping overnight in the parking lot or waiting in line for hours to be one of the first to get a newly released phone?

You go to Disneyland for an experience, not a commodity, and the theme parks foster this concept. Disneyland welcomes guests, never customers, and has a cast, not employees.

Thanks to an ingenuous marketing technique, Geek Squad generates more than a billion dollars a year in revenue. The technicians do the same job as other computer repair services. However, the branded VW Beetle, black slacks and white shirt uniform, pocket protector, and thin, black tie, turns the repair visit into a fun experience.

MAXIMUM CUSTOMER EXPERIENCE

——————————— =

MINIMUM VARIATION

GREAT CUSTOMER APPRECIATION

Goods and services are no longer enough. People are looking for experience and will pay a premium for it. Business and products have gone from something you want to something you love to something you experience. I love experiential services because that is how I learn. This also seems to be a growing trend in our society. People are becoming hyper-stimulated by technology, and just watching is boring. What can you do to make your business more fun/involved/interactive for those that are customers? This will define your DyVal.

For the Greater Good

Having a vision, a plan, and a purpose is noble, but it is not enough. Knowing your motives is crucial. Simon Sineck, author of *Start with Why* calls it "aligning in your why." It is critical to know that we are aligned in a positive way in our personal and business relationships.

A wake-up call for me came when I owned a Keller Williams franchise. It was an ego trip for me to say that I owned a franchise with four offices. If you peeled back my motives as you would the layers of an onion, you would have seen that pride was at the core. Yes, I wanted to help other realtors become successful. I also wanted to make more money as an owner and to tell people that I owned a company instead of saying that I was just a realtor.

My belief in the procession process and my mantra of *everything is perfect* helped me to emotionally survive when my partners sold our franchise to a competitor. Losing that business allowed me the time, money, and resources to pursue other opportunities in which I could become aligned in my greater calling. We don't get to choose what happens to us; we only get to choose how we deal with what happens to us. I learned that through financial success or financial loss. I am only a steward of the gifts and talents and monetary blessings that have been entrusted to me.

One way to focus that works for me is to create a vision board. Mine is in my office. Creating a vision board simply means that you put up pictures of what you want and written intentions of what you want to achieve. Maybe you stick a picture of the Eiffel Tower up because you want to visit Paris or one of Mickey Mouse because you've never been to Disneyland. You might envision a new car or boat or being self-employed. Whatever you want to create goes on the board. The big caveat with a vision board is that you must attach every vision picture, note, and dream with intention.

Go to bed and wake up with gratitude. Before you close your eyes at night think of at least one thing you are grateful for. Before your feet hit the ground think of at least one thing you are grateful for. By doing this simple task, I believe you will sleep better because you will be at peace with everything. When you start your day with a positive outlook, it will have a positive effect all day. Going to bed stressed over what might be left on your to-do list or waking up stressed over what you have to achieve only creates more stress. I believe even people who are going through tough times or are battling depression can benefit from this ritual. As so many people say, "What you focus on expands," so _choose your focus wisely._

Abundant Vision

Below is an exercise to practice analyzing abundant vision. Take a few minutes to consider these questions and jot down your ideas.

1. How far in the future are you planning your vision? Do your short-term intentions tie into your long-term intentions?

_____

_____

2. What could you change in your business that would allow your customers to have a more interactive or experiential experience?

_____

_____

_____

_____

3. Who is your mentor or second opinion? Is there another person that you could add to invest in your decision-making process?

_____

_____

_____

Your vision keeps you in motion. While you may deviate from your path from time to time, it is important that you have your ultimate intention in mind. As Steven Covey, author of _7 Habits of Highly Effective People_, says, "The main thing is to keep the main thing the main thing."

CHAPTER FIVE
ABUNDANT GROWTH

Think of a time when you had a period of amazing growth in your business or personal life. I'll bet that before the growth, you experienced a significant struggle or challenge that you overcame. Am I right?

One of the most frequent questions I get asked is how I became a serial entrepreneur. Were my parents business owners or entrepreneurs? Were my parents investors? Did I have a successful grandpa or uncle that taught me everything I know? The answer to all these questions is no.

To this day, my parents are very risk adverse. By the time I was 20, I had bought more real estate than they had bought in their entire lives. So how did I become who I am and create this growth mindset at a young age without business direction from my parents?

One thing I knew, and which I already stated, was that I did not want to have to struggle as they had. Another is that I have always loved to learn, to try new things, and push myself to limits that others thought were impossible. A huge motivator was being told by my teachers or anyone else that I could *not* accomplish something. That always pushed me to do whatever it took to prove them wrong.

I once visited a local realtor who had more foreclosures listed than anyone in the area. I can still see him sitting behind his desk that was piled high with four stacks of papers, each stack about eighteen-inches high. When I told him that I was considering getting into the foreclosure business, he leaned back in his chair, clasped his hands across his stomach, and said, "Well, bring it on."

"Every year, many people say they are going to do it only to find out how hard it is to get into the business," he continued. "If they are lucky enough to get in, they have to manage to hold on to their accounts."

In that moment, I felt as if he did not think I was capable of succeeding, and that he was mocking me. Every new client I got brought me closer to getting into the business, I desired. I also told him, "I'm going to have the top spot." Not too long later, I took the number one spot away from him along with lots of his clients and never looked back.

I chose not to pursue a formal education. Formal schooling just wasn't for me especially being dyslexic. Not saying formal education is right or wrong just not right for me. Plenty of highly successful people have gone to college. Plenty of them are still waiting tables or bartending because they can make more money and work fewer hours. The same is true for on-the-job learners like me. They range from successful millionaires to those who are barely scraping by. This is the great part about life. By thinking and acting abundantly, you can achieve success regardless of your education.

I have an honorable double major in the school of hard knocks, and I have spent hundreds of thousands of dollars on that education. I have also paid hundreds of thousands of dollars on specific training and personal development. I have just chosen to spend my education dollars in a different fashion than most; sometimes in a new business venture that lost every penny I invested. This and most of these lessons, while trying, were highly educational. I have said I will never lose; I will either win or learn. Both are true gifts. During the times my life was easy, I do not think I was learning or growing much. One of those periods just happened over the last few months of me writing this. Those times challenge me to evaluate what I am doing to see if there is a way to push myself.

Push Your Limits

From a world perspective, my life is great. I have an amazing wife, two fabulous daughters, excellent health, and a handful of prospering businesses. However, I felt as though I was not learning or pushing myself. Although I am living the American dream, when I look in the mirror I have to ask myself whether or not I am living up to my highest God-given potential.

During this time, I felt as if I were in no man's land, not happy about what I was doing but not unhappy. This is a dangerous place to be because we are not going to experience growth by being comfortable. Only by confronting our most difficult struggles do we find our greatest strengths and possibilities. If we do not try, we will never know what we are truly capable of.

When I began to invest in real estate, oil and gas-exploration, and manufacturing, I knew nothing about these industries. I had a choice, as we all do each time we want to achieve a desire. I could let fear paralyze me and let my mind wander into the scarcity of telling myself that I might not be good enough; or worse, that I did not deserve to try because I was too stupid to learn about these industries. Or I could choose to swallow my pride, and ask for help. As I sat in meetings with people who had made fortunes in these industries, I humbled myself and asked a lot of questions. You should too. Many people do not ask questions for fear of sounding ignorant. For that reason, they often miss huge opportunities to learn. Remember, most people love to share what they know.

Throughout life, we have dozens of opportunities to either fight and overcome or take our ball and go home. Because it was a difficult experience in which I was often uncomfortable, I could have chosen to give up. Instead, I chose to climb over each wall until I was through the obstacle course and had learned a new trade.

Everyone lives by different standards. Mine are to never get too comfortable, and always push the bar. I know people who have far more or far less than I, and each one must experience this personal process. Whether you realize it or not, choosing nothing is also a choice.

Any challenge in life can be scary. However, when I look back on a challenge I overcame, I can still feel the thrill of pushing through it and see how I grew as a person. So I ask you, what is worse than doing things wrong? It is doing things right that do not need to be done or those that do not really matter. When you do things wrong you can gain insight and knowledge to achieve greater goals. If you don't try those things, you will never know what you missed. Remember, anything worth doing is worth doing wrong for a while so you can learn.

Feeding the Alligators

I had just quit a well-paying corporate job and was buying real estate as fast as possible because of the low interest stated income adjustable-rate mortgages that were available. As I had no steady income, the bills began to pile up. Then, the interest rates began to adjust upward. Soon, the house payments that had begun at $1,000 a month were now $1,500 a month.

That was a lot of alligators, a term I use for any property that can eat you alive but must be fed every month. This type of investment is commonly called negative property or negative cash flow property, which means more dollars are going out than rental income brings in.

At the time, I owned about a dozen homes. Five hundred extra dollars per house for twelve homes equaled an additional $6,000 monthly cost that was gone before I could even attempt to pay any personal bills. You do not need a degree in finance to understand this is not a good situation. I remember thinking that I would have to short-sale these houses or possibly even lose them through foreclosure.

I remember telling my wife that the next six months were going to be very interesting. We had two options. File bankruptcy, or manage to fight through the crisis and end up with a very nice income for us in the future. Personally, I had two choices. Go in my office, cry, and beat myself up about why I bought all these homes or got stupid adjustable rate loans during the subprime times, or be a man of integrity and pay the banks the money as I had agreed and fight to get out of this hole.

I chose to fight and keep my integrity intact. Over the next six months, I worked harder and longer hours trying to put deals together then I ever had. Those months were tight, and we were not comfortable at all. I had to start making decisions about what I needed and what I wanted when I was shopping or about to spend any money. However, working through it and coming out the other side was a true gift. Going through that time has allowed me to experience what many in the world are living on a regular basis. I can see how staying in this position for a long period of time would cloud your judgment and effect your ability to push forward.

From Average to Great

The difference between average and great is the ability to deliver predictable products and services. Most businesses are not consistent, and that is why they fail. They continue to hire and fire staff with the same broken system in place. Did you know that 94% of the breakdown is in the system? That means only 6% of either failure or success is with the people.

Most franchises make money by selling a system. Look at McDonald's, probably one of the most hated fast food companies in the world. However, it is successful because it has a system in place. They sell $27 billion dollars a year of mediocre burgers and fries. However, people go there because it is consistent—two pickles, a quarter ounce of ketchup, the same meat, bun, and sauce whether you are in the US, China, or anywhere else in the world.

People like to buy franchises because you are buying a pre-validated system instead of building one from scratch through trial and error. These trials and errors take time and normally a lot of money. By skipping this learning process, you are able to get right to business. Normally, in a franchise, the margins are a little tighter because you have to share profits or pay a franchise fee monthly, but if you start a company and your system isn't right, you can have the pleasure of owning 100% of a failing business.

As they say, good enough never is. If you are considering starting a business, the first 20% is where the business is made or lost. This includes the underlying theory and context that everything has to fit within. This is where the planning and validating your plan starts to happen. A lot of startups think they have a good idea, and then try to build the company around the idea. Ninety percent fail because they run out of good ideas or funds because they did not get the first 20% right.

If you have an idea, take the time to validate that idea. See if there are other products on the market that are competing against yours. What makes theirs good? More important, what makes yours better? If there is no product like yours on the market, the next question should be does anyone even want what you have to sell?

There are some exceptions, like the Pet Rock. Anyone in their right mind would say no one wants that, but we know people did. Conduct some market surveys and consult people in the industry to see if there is a need. If there is, research what it will cost to develop and sell. What is the customer willing to pay for this product or service?

Remember, success leaves clues, so find people in the space and get a mentor. Am I driving getting a mentor or coach home hard enough for you? Okay, good! It will save you so much time and money because very few ideas are new. If you find someone that has been in business long enough, chances are very high they have seen your idea and will have a better solution than you can come up with. If nothing else, they can tell you what didn't work and you can learn from that so you can avoid those trials.

I was at lunch with a very successful friend of mine who is worth many millions of dollars. I asked him about his secret to success. His reply was simple but very profound.

"Do what you know, know what you do, and strive to know more."

He is focused on two industries and has done very well for himself. If you ask him what stocks he likes, he will look at you like you are a crazy man. He does not buy stocks because that is not what he knows. I had to learn this lesson the hard way. I don't specialize in stock trading, so I should have never done it. I thought I was going to invest in some stocks that I thought were going to be great. The market taught me that the stocks I picked weren't good, and I lost around $50,000 in a matter of a week.

Strive to know more. Dive into industry publications, go to conferences, see what the new trends are, do research, and study. This can be knowledge on your specialty or other industries that could influence your space. Network at conferences to build your knowledge. Remember that your network is your net worth.

Sometimes it is smart to quit because you aren't getting results or the leverage you wanted. At the time, I was embracing the idea of never, ever quitting and always battling my way to the top. Little did I know that being stubborn was actually holding me back from success.

If I asked you to name someone who failed in business, was defeated for state legislature, whose sweetheart died, had a nervous breakdown, was defeated for house speaker and Congress, rejected for land office, defeated for US Senate, defeated for Vice President nomination, and again defeated for US Senate, I think that most of you would think this person was a mad man and should have given up. That was the great Abraham Lincoln's journey.

With so much failure and disappointment, most people would have given up, but he fought on to become one of the greatest leaders of all time and the president of the United States.

The secret is learning when you are in the dip and about to catapult forward and when you are at a dead end and need to quit. Having a team that can help you to identify the difference between the two is very important. People thought the Wright brothers were crazy, but they took a chance and pushed through when everyone else told them they were wrong.

When I was in food sales, I wanted to earn a large customer's business. I would go into the restaurant once a week and bring him a food sample or a flyer, then thank him for his time and leave him a card that he would rip up and throw away in the trashcan right in front of me. He would always go on about my company and how bad an experience he'd had with us in the past.

Despite the horror stories people told me, I was determined to get this account. I was going to show everyone that I could land it. I went back to this same account the same time every week for a couple of months and went through the same drill: give him something and give him a card to rip up and throw away.

To some, this would have been a sign to quit and move on to the other accounts that would have been more respectful and more receptive to my message. However, I felt that I was in a dip and about to break through. One day before I called on him, I decided on a new approach because my current method surely was not working. That day I had my business card laminated so no matter what happened, he would not be able to rip it up. As usual, I walked into the restaurant with food samples and did my usual I-would-love-an-opportunity-to-earn-your-business pitch. I could barely get my speech out because I was so excited to see his face when I handed him my laminated card.

Finally, the moment came when he said he hated us and would never do business with us. I gave this very serious, older gentleman who had been brutal to me my laminated card. He burst out laughing and said, "You are a persistent little bastard."

"I am absolutely persistent," I agreed. "And I will keep coming back until you give me a chance to prove that I can give you great service."

He smiled and said, "Come back next week, and I will give you an inventory list so we can see what can be done."

I ended up getting his business in both his locations, and this became one of my favorite accounts because of the struggle it took to get it.

We all are going to have road blocks, but what are we going to do different to set ourselves apart from the others? By answering this question, you will help define your abundant growth plan.

CHAPTER SIX
FINANCIAL ABUNDANCE

I have been blessed to make a lot of money. I have also lost as much as hundreds of thousands of dollars in a single afternoon. I don't say this to boast or beg pity, as it isn't cool; it's just reality for me. Instead of falling apart and telling myself that I was stupid for making an unsound investment, I went home and had dinner with my family as usual. I believed that something much bigger had just happened, and there was a lesson to learn. Although some lessons were cheap and came with a warning, others were very expensive and dropped on me like a pallet of bricks.

Losing that kind of money didn't feel good. I was never excited about it. Most people have a totally different reaction. *I can't do it. I am not good enough*. However, I believe that because I kept the "*It's perfect*" mentality versus crying in my Cheerios, I have attracted many more opportunities.

Winning the Lottery is not About Abundance

We've all read stories of people who have won millions of dollars in a lottery, only to be broke within a few years. They lose everything, including their closest relationships.

I knew someone who won the Colorado lottery two times within a three-year period. From the outside, his life looked good because he was rolling in cash. Sadly, he ended up committing suicide because his life wasn't as good as we all assumed. His wife ended up having an affair with one of his business partners. Money doesn't always bring you happiness.

According to *CNNMoney* in 2014, Americans spent more than $70 billion on lottery tickets. Furthermore, those households with less than $13,000 in income spent an average of $645, or 9% of that income on the lottery.

Nine percent of anyone's annual income placed in a safe investment will grow into a substantial amount over time. Nine percent in a regular low-interest savings account at the bank would provide funds for emergencies.

Buying lottery tickets is another example of operating from emotional scarcity. Instead of taking action to invest the money or spend it on education or in some way that results in more opportunity, the scarcity mind sits on the couch and hopes that Lady Luck will drop a truckload of cash in its lap.

When you take action, you are living fully. You experience all the true gifts that life brings. When you deny yourself those experiences because of fear and anxiety, you miss the abundance that's all around you. When you are operating in fear, you aren't yourself. We are never at our best when we are in fear.

The scarcity-minded person sits and cries, "My life sucks. I need to go buy lotto tickets. Hopefully, I will win." They wait for someone else to give them what they already have the power to create.

Let's do a mental exercise. Do you want to know what it feels like to be a millionaire? Okay, get comfortable. Uncross your legs and arms, and close your eyes. Imagine yourself as a millionaire and that you have everything you want and desire that money can buy. Take a few minutes to set this scene in your head. Now open your eyes. How do you feel? Do you feel a change in you as a person? Or do you feel the same as before your daydream? Millionaires do not feel any different than the rest of the people. Money might give you more options in life, but you are still the same person. I thought one day I would wake up and say, "Wow, this feels really good." The fact is that it feels the same; you just have a different set of problems to deal with. I know millionaires and even billionaires, and I can tell you that, at the end of the day, they are all just people.

Sharing is Having More

Competition is a worldview of scarcity. Peter Thiel, co-founder of PayPal and Venture Capital Hedge Fund manager, says, "In the convergent worldview, competition is a relic of history." Cooperation has a worldview of abundance. Sharing generates having more. It creates energy, is far less stressful, and makes it more fun to work with others. A great example of this is Ford, GM, and Chrysler, companies with the scarcity mindset, and Tesla Motors, a company with an abundant mindset.

Tesla Motors, run by billionaire Elon Musk, is the fastest production electric car on the market today, going from 0-60 in 2.8 seconds. To put that in prospective, a new Corvette goes 0-60 in 3.6 seconds on fuel. Tesla also has the longest range on a full charge and tons of other great technologies. Tesla wants to cooperate and share proprietary secrets through open source so everyone can advance faster. Open source refers to any program whose source code is made available for use or modification as users or other developers see fit. Tesla is willing to give away all its great big ideas through a process called open code. The big three in the auto industry want to compete against each other. In the 2009 auto bailout, Tesla got zero dollars and the big three—Ford, GM, and Chrysler—shared more than $80 billion in bailout money. Chrysler and GM ultimately ended up filling bankruptcy even after all the bail out money they received.

Think how fast we could move forward if we all worked together like Tesla. If other manufacturers could come up to Tesla's standards of innovation and sharing, the auto industry could move forward exponentially. Why does every company need to build a transmission for a car? Why can't one company make a really good one and share it with others? Then make a great engine and share that with others. This thinking might sound crazy to some, but this is the shift we must make to move forward. GM and Ford are laying off engineers because with Tesla having open code they just copy what the innovators are doing. So why don't they share the great things they are working on as well so everyone can grow faster instead of 10 companies working to solve the same problem?

Instead, competition prevents sharing of information for fear everyone will make similarly good products. That makes the industry move forward as if driving through mud. These scarcity examples exist in every industry.

One that particularly bothers me is the pharmaceutical industry. These people are competing against each other, and killing hundreds of thousands of people along the way, because they refuse to share. If they would share their technology and research resources, medicine would advance so fast that it would literally change the world. Instead, the pharmaceutical companies hide their secrets in order to make billions at the cost of humanity and thousands and thousands of lives. If they could figure out who was the farthest along in a cure and add to that research instead of replicating, we could cure cancer and so many other terrible diseases.

Sharing creates more personal abundance as well. While at a class taught by my now-mentor, Marshall Thurber, in Colorado, a college-age young man came in and sat next to me. He looked very tired and didn't exactly smell pleasant.

One of the things Marshall teaches is that you need to have snacks and protein throughout the training sessions in order to operate at optimal performance. Marshall's team would set a table with a variety of nutritious foods such as apples, granola bars, and peanuts, which we could eat during the breaks. During the first break, this guy grabbed a couple of apples and a handful of granola bars. He obviously hadn't eaten, and I was drawn to hear his story.

At the first break, I was able to talk to this person and hear a little of his story. It turns out that one of his friends had taken Marshall's class in the past, recommended it, and had even asked the guy's father to pay this young man's way. His friend's dad agreed, and that's why he was attending. We had lunch together that day, and I started to learn more about him. At the time, he was living in his friend's garage. Not inside the house, but in a garage...in Colorado...in the winter.

He told me that his father was very controlling and wanted him to finish college and go into the business field. This man was rebelling and thinking about going to art school in San Francisco because he knew that would make his father mad. We had a nice time together, and I suggested that he come to another one of Marshall's seminars that I had taken previously because I thought it would be truly transformational. I think the tuition was about $1,000 for the next seminar.

He said, "That sounds great, but I don't have the money."

I felt compelled to get him in the class, so I told him, "Show up in the morning, and I will take care of it for you."

He didn't have a job, so I knew his schedule was wide open at the time and he could make the time work. He had a great experience with the course and was very thankful for the gift from me. About three weeks later, I received the following email.

Hey Justin,

I thought I would check in with you and let you know I am signed up for classes at CSU. With me playing full out, I will be finishing a business degree in one year. Another big thing for me is that I have been sober since the game that we played in Marshall's class. While I have gotten on and off the wagon before, this time it feels different. I hope you had a great holiday with your family.

Since then, I have had a couple of lunches and phone calls with him to stay in touch and help to keep him on a better track. He is no longer homeless and living in someone's garage. He was recently studying abroad in China and loving the learning experience. His drinking is still under control, and he told me that he found a girl he thinks is the one.

By me being aware of another's needs and having abundance to share, I helped this young man move from a destructive life of hating his father and trying to drink his pain away to not only sleeping under a roof, but under a roof in China because he was following his dreams. He has found love and is now moving to California. There are so many people hurting in this world who only want someone to care about them.

If we can take time and resources out of our life because we are operating in abundance, we can truly make great changes in others and in the world. In this particular situation, I was able to see the outcome and stay in contact with him. Sometimes we help people and we don't see the actual fruit, but we should plant the seeds anyway. Our act might transition someone's life, but we may never know.

Although that is a great story, the point is to share what you have regardless of the outcome. I cannot control his long-term success. Only he can do that. Even if he had not chosen to change his life, I still would have felt that I had done the right thing.

With a strong trend towards the scarcity mindset in both personal and professional lives, many focus on keeping success to themselves. Potentially, a mindset of sharing could produce exponential growth and progress for all.

There is No Secret

The movie *The Secret* sold millions of copies. Although based on setting intentions, it only told half the theory. Yes, you have to think positive and set good intentions to succeed, but you also must take action.

My experience has been that sitting on the couch dreaming about owning a Ferrari will not get me a Ferrari. By setting good intentions and believing there is enough, and working for what we want, we can rest assured that more deals and opportunities will come.

This type of wishful thinking creates less abundance and feeds the scarcity mindset. Say that you intend to make a million dollars, and you think about it for a week or two but that's all you do. You are not taking any action to actually make this dream come true. Then you get discouraged because this doesn't work either. This is another scarcity mindset that sets up the unrealistic expectation that all you have to do is intend for something good to happen and it happens.

By setting good intentions and believing there is an abundance of deals or opportunities, your real goal focuses on making everyone happy. When you are in a scarcity mindset, you squeeze the deal so hard to get every penny out of it that the other person doesn't feel good. While you might have gotten a little more out of the deal by squeezing, you might sacrifice opportunities to work with that person on future deals.

You will also damage your reputation. When we operate from a scarcity mindset, it becomes easier to let our integrity slide. When we are desperate for money, we will make different choices than when we believe there is enough and that we don't have to compromise our beliefs to reach a goal. For me, integrity is the essence of everything. If you have integrity, nothing else matters. If you don't have integrity, nothing else matters.

Honesty is often used as a synonym for integrity, but integrity is a more comprehensive virtue. While it is partly about honesty, it goes beyond just telling the truth. Integrity has the same root as integer which means wholeness. It includes authenticity, fairness, trustworthiness, and moral courage. It involves doing what we believe is right based on our values and the right thing to do regardless of the circumstances, even when it may involve a substantial personal cost. We don't need be a hero or a saint to have high integrity. Integrity isn't particularly common or rare in life. Everyone can and should aspire to integrity in their own personal lives.

Jeffrey Skilling, the ex-CEO of Enron Corp, didn't have integrity. Enron Corp is a company that reached crazy heights. Many know how the story ends with the bankruptcy of one of America's largest corporations. Enron's collapse affected the lives of 20,000 employees and shook Wall Street. At Enron's peak, its price per share was $90.75; it was said to be worth $111 billion during 2000. Forbes named Enron "America's Most Innovative Company" for six consecutive years. In 2002, Enron Corp's stock price plummeted to $0.67 following bankruptcy and a total liquidation. To this day, many wonder how such a powerful business disintegrated almost overnight and how it managed to fool the regulators with fake, off-the-books corporations for so long. CEO Jeffrey Skilling didn't wake up one day and say *I am going to trash my reputation and cheat hundreds of thousands of innocent people out of billions of their hard-earned dollars.*

Skilling had a review process where he would fire the bottom 15% of the company each year based on performance. They called it the rank and yank system. Skilling thought it was the company's most important strategy to be the best. What he wasn't accounting for was that this promoted deception and discouraged integrity. People were lying about their performance to try and save their jobs. This created a culture of propping up numbers to make people look good.

Somethings starts with a small lie. Then it begins to slowly compound until it snowballs. At the time, it does not feel big, but your integrity slowly slips away. Eventually, you find yourself in a deep hole and have to lie just to keep going until the music stops and you are exposed. This isn't saying that every small decision or white lie is going to cause an Enron-size disaster, but they certainly add up.

One way to make staying in integrity easier is to try not to make decisions when you are on the bottom or when you are going through an emotional time. This is especially important when making major life decisions such as career changes and in relationships. But it is also applicable to everyday situations as well. Take some time and listen to the people whose opinions you value, especially those who will not automatically agree with you.

In the book *Decisive: How to Make Better Choices in Life and Work,* by Chip Heath and Dan Heath, there is talk about how important diversity is unless you are in a highly-specialized field. A brain surgeon is highly specialized and spends hours to master his craft. However, the 10,000-hour rule only applies to specialists or maybe professional athletes that train that many hours. Other than those circumstances, a diverse group will always outperform a single individual.

We all have biases, and we like to surround ourselves with people who support our ideas or confirm our biases. This will not serve anyone. We should actually get people who are the most diverse from us to help us see our challenges and our blind spots. We typically do not choose people who will ask the hard questions because that creates tension. However, this is what we need the most to find the best solutions.

Instead, we want to surround ourselves with people who agree with us and tell us we are brilliant. Although I like positive reinforcement as much as the next guy, the most helpful comments I receive are honest and candid, especially if they are different from my thoughts. These can reveal the true value of our ideas and make us question why we assumed we were right.

Each person has had a different set of experiences that bring a unique perspective to any situation. Attachment to our ideas and biases will never help us make the best decisions. I encourage you to seek diversity in age, gender, occupation, even wealth when making decisions. All of these perspectives will help you to challenge assumptions and common beliefs, especially if you are getting ready to launch a new product. Your test group should be very diverse. You can focus energy on your target client, but the feedback you receive from a diverse group could help you sell even more to the target audience.

I have thought a property or an idea was great until I bounced it off my business partners, my spouse, my colleagues, my brother, and my friends only to discover that I had overlooked a minor, or sometimes major, issue. Over the years, this single act has saved me millions of dollars.

By operating from an abundant finance mentality, you should not feel threatened by bringing others into deals and giving them a piece of the pie. You will understand that together we are better. We should learn to listen more and hold our ideas loose in our hands. Sometimes success is so blinding that we do not see how the environment is changing around us because we think we can't be beaten.

Look at the film and imaging giant Kodak. They were so successful that they ignored the shift to digital cameras. By the time the company realized that using film and printing pictures were becoming virtually obsolete and tried to shift, it was too late.

For more than 110 years, Kodak had a rich history of being the leader in the film industry. In 1877, Founder George Eastman's goal was "to make the camera as convenient as the pencil". He was on the cutting edge of reducing the size and weight so people could take cameras on vacations. As the years went on,

Kodak quit being the innovator and did not want to cannibalize its extremely lucrative gross margins of its global domination. With almost 90% market share of film sales and 85% of camera sales, they were very comfortable. Kodak was doing $16 billion in sales with 145,000 employees worldwide in 1988. Steven Sasson, the Kodak engineer who invented the first digital camera in 1975, characterized the initial corporate response to his invention this way, "It was filmless photography, so management's reaction was, 'That's cute—but don't tell anyone about it.'"

Instead of saying, "Let's use this to our benefit and get in front of the curve," management hid it and did nothing but push their high-margin goods. Any new technology has fierce competition, low margins, and cannibalizes your high-margin core business. Kodak did not take decisive action to combat the inevitable challenges. Keep in mind, at the time this company was flush with cash and could have invested millions on the technology without feeling it in the bottom line. They could have bought some startups that already had some concepts they could build on. This is called the innovators dilemma, where a company doesn't want to innovate because of the fear of cannibalizing their own product. As we know now, companies like Sony took the opportunity to invest in the new technology and Kodak filed for bankruptcy in January, 2012. A structural change will not go away. It is like someone saying they will keep their slow horse instead of drive around in an efficient car—it isn't going to happen. The change is here, and it is here to stay.

Another example is Blockbuster, a huge video rental company. Their chance to shift was handed to them on a silver platter, and they turned it down. In 2000, Reed Hastings, the founder of what became Netflix, attempted to talk to Blockbuster CEO, John Antioco.

Hastings suggested a partnership between Netflix and Blockbuster. Netflix would manage the online brand and Blockbuster would retain the retail stores. Hastings got laughed out of the conference room. Although his idea was great, he didn't have a big enough market share to capture the movie rental giant's interest.

In 2004, Blockbuster was valued at $5 billion and had more than 60,000 employees. In 2010, the company went bankrupt because so many people were getting videos from sources like Netflix and Red Box. Netflix is now worth $32 billion.

Blockbuster and John Antioco didn't want to share some of their pie. Today, half of that $32 billion pie would have been worth three times their largest market valuation.

There are dozens of companies like Kodak and Blockbuster that had a scarcity mindset, refused to share, and ended up losing everything.

Closer to home, a friend of mine owns a major local construction company. They generated about $150 million a year in business and employed 250 people and many hundreds of subcontractors. On the outside, the business looked amazing, and money poured in. In fact, it was going so well that my friend, the founder, had actually stepped out of the business and hired a CEO to take his place. Then a problem appeared.

In 2010, after one of their structural engineers had signed off on a building design for a school in Colorado, a precast wall in the gym settled three inches due to an improperly installed U-joint that slipped out of place. My friend ordered a peer review to make sure there were no additional issues. In 2011, peer review recommended closing the school, as it was unsafe for students. This was a brand-new school that had only been open for one year.

During the peer review, the reviewers discovered that the engineer's license had lapsed during the time of his design. This triggered an audit and another peer review of the school building to make sure it met the current state building codes. The auditors found a couple of areas that did not meet code. This discovery sent the town where the school was located into immediate panic.

As you can imagine, people thought the school and the children who were attending weren't safe. Of course, that sounded bad, but the problem could be fixed.

My friend had been a successful business owner whose success had blinded him from checking all the details. With his level of success, he delegated more of his duties instead of doing them himself. After interviewing him, the *Denver Post* ran a front-page article, *School Unsafe, Unsound*. As the story hit the news and got a lot of press, more school administrators and owners of other buildings his company had built started to call and ask for peer reviews. Each peer review averaged $35,000 to $40,000 to have another structural engineer check calculations and see if they would have done anything differently on the building. In total, 94 structures were reviewed, and 74 were found to have defects that needed repairs. These buildings ranged from commercial buildings to schools and hospitals.

As you can imagine, there are lots of opinions on how to interpret the code, so many reviews came back with suggestions for a number of expensive fixes. Now, my friend had to make some tough choices. New jobs they were bidding on started to pull deals back because they were uncertain of the company's future. He now had to get back in his company and start doing triage. He sold assets to keep up with the bills and lay off staff because with no new work coming in, he could no longer afford them. The company's annual budget was slashed by two thirds from $9.5 million to $3.5 million. At the same time, they had massive work and expenses on the buildings being reviewed. Bottom line; he had to lay off about 150 of his 250 employees and spent almost $14 million correcting problems. Of the $14 million, $9 million came from company funds, and both the owners had to write personal checks for $2.5 million each to cover the short fall to repair the problems. They also had to restructure and obtain loans to get them through the difficult time.

After losing basically everything, he had to start over. You know that he learned a hard lesson as he watched his company's revenue drop from $150 million to $40 million. Because he thought his company was running smoothly, he stopped pushing to make it even better and lost nearly everything he had. However, he not only rebuilt his business, but because of his integrity and the fact that he took responsibility for these problems, he ended up receiving the American Business Ethics Award. For the first time in history, the 30-person award committee unanimously approved a company.

Today, my friend's company leads the industry in peer reviews with a procedure designed to conduct internal reviews on every product used within the construction process. In addition, a system of quality control checks is in place that assures the integrity of the materials from order to delivery.

The secret is that you must take action and be aware of industry changes. Part of the greatest thing is having diversity to highlight your blind spots, which may help alleviate the possibility of getting left behind in trends.

Don't Become Complacent

Being successful is wonderful. However, you can also get lazy and take things for granted. You become complacent and stop challenging yourself. Sometimes pride or ego keeps us from asking the really important questions we need to know to learn. We want people to think that we are successful so we do not ask others' opinions because we are too proud. We may also think they will think we are stupid if we ask too many questions.

What small things are you letting slip or not finding a better way to do? What questions could you ask to push yourself farther? Who could help you catapult your business to the next level?

When we are green and young in a business, we ask lots of questions so we can learn. Do not let this habit fall away even if you are working on your tenth business. Live like the new intern or the new hire in a company. Instead of letting pride get in the way, we need to become humble, hungry leaders again. Think back to when you were new at something. How did you solve the problem? Did you get resourceful? How did you feel? With knowledge, we start to make assumptions and begin to miss things.

What are you, a knower or a learner? A knower thinks they know everything and doesn't ask questions or try to learn more. A learner is someone who is seeking to learn and understand all the time. Look at some of the companies that thought they were so smart. Kodak, the world's largest printing and imaging company, thought they were the best. They quit asking questions, and worse they quit listening to smart people around them. Because they didn't listen to others, they did not see the new trends that were coming or disruptive forces that could wreck them. They became a knower instead of a learner and paid dearly for that mistake. Digital cameras and photos on phones would destroy their business because they didn't adapt.

When we are new at a job, we work harder and faster because we want to ease our tension as quickly as possible. When we are big, fat, and happy, we are slow to change and adapt because we are comfortable and have no urgency to move. Are we learning and growing when we are in the comfort zone? True abundance comes when you are reaching for the next rung of the ladder, whatever that is in your world. That will give you more knowledge and/or resources you can share with others.

Here are some habits that have served me well:

1. **Periodically throw away your notes so you are forced to rebuild.** How many people repeat the same comfortable speech, lesson plan, or presentation because it is easy? When you do this, both you and the people you are trying to reach miss out on the latest innovations and new trends.

Both Jeff Bezos, CEO of Amazon, and Jeff Weiner, CEO of LinkedIn, have eliminated PowerPoint presentations from their meetings. This forces the presenters to not use crutches like PowerPoint so presentations are more engaging.

2. **Always speak your truth, even if the rest of the group isn't on board with the decision.** My mentor, Marshall Thurber, always invites me to meetings because I speak my truth, even if it isn't popular. This doesn't mean that we always disagree or that I am always right, but it starts a conversation and dialogue that can lead to a better answer or solution than we had initially. Sitting silent does not serve anyone.

3. **Be vulnerable.** You must learn that it is okay if you do not know something, and it is okay to say that you do not know. Too many people try to fake it until they make it, which usually involves a lot of lying. By being vulnerable, you will be more open to learning. More important, you will possibly save yourself from a major costly mistake like we talked about earlier.

   Vulnerability is the core of fear, shame, and the struggle out of feeling worthless. Vulnerability is also the birthplace of joy and worthiness and growth.

4. **You do not have to be the leader on every project.** Sometimes taking a support role and letting someone else lead brings fresh ideas that we otherwise would have missed. Letting others take the lead will also help boost morale as you empower employees and others to drive things forward. As leaders, we sometimes forget that great things can happen when we give the wheel to someone else.

More times than I care to admit, I have stepped down as a leader and given someone else the wheel only to discover they did a much better job than I. Me and my pride were the only things that had slowed down the project.

5. **Seek help from people who are successful in your area.** No matter how big your company is or how smart you think you are, you should always have a couple of mentors and probably a coach. Recently, I asked one of my mentors if I could intern in his company. He was surprised and laughed at me.

"Become an intern? What are you talking about? You're a multimillionaire."

"I'm serious," I told him. "I want to learn about your company from the bottom up."

He was ultra-successful, and I had to swallow my pride to ask to be considered for the lowest position in his firm. You might think going back to an entry-level position was a crazy idea because I seemingly had it made. I actually debated if I should write that I am a multimillionaire in this book. I strive to be humble so I struggled with leaving it in, but I wanted to drive the point home that it is never too late to go back to learning. I see it as a huge gift to be able to go back to being an intern, asking questions, and learning from a master in his space.

I do not know exactly how it is all going to play out, but I think it will be one of the greatest learning experiences of my life. The combination of the experience I have and the knowledge I will receive is a great formula for abundant growth in my future.

One of my favorite sayings is, "What questions would you ask that could transform your life beyond your wildest dreams?" What questions or requests are you not asking/making that could transform your life? Whom could you ask to mentor you? Are you living a life of pride or a life of humility? So many people go through life not asking for help, especially wealthy or highly successful people. I know there are times I don't think highly successful people would have time to meet with me, or maybe I don't deserve their time. But now I always ask regardless of whether or not it is comfortable.

I was at a business meeting with lots of successful people for a private bank function where Steve Wozniak, co-founder of Apple, was speaking on technology. When he was done, everyone was staring at him in awe. I wanted a picture with him, so I got out of my chair, walked up to him, introduced myself, and asked if I could get a picture. Before he answered, I was already pulling my phone out and turning to take a selfie with him. He might have said no, but I would have gone home knowing I at least asked. He was very gracious and took a photo with me. So many people would have loved a picture with him but took no action to get what they wanted!

I think deep inside, we know the questions but are afraid to ask for help. If you knew a person who had the expertise to transform your life, wouldn't that be worth a phone call? It has been my experience that most people are happy to help and feel honored to be considered. These vulnerable requests may impact the course of your life more than you can imagine, but you must make them. Once you have figured out what it is you want to do, then take some action to move forward.

Although no one knows exactly who said it first, one of my favorite sayings is, "Your best thinking got you to exactly where you are today." Einstein put it this way, "We cannot solve our problems with the same level of thinking it took to create them." For some of us, this is good. For others, this is a tough pill to swallow. You would not knowingly sabotage your life, right? Your best thoughts got you in all the bad situations you have experienced. That is why we need to surround ourselves with smart people and diversity to help us take our thinking to the next level. I think the greatest wealth is buried in cemeteries across the world. Can you imagine the cumulative brain power in the minds of all those who have gone before us? With this in mind, take advantage of those around you, and ask questions so you can benefit from their knowledge.

A lot of people have said that we are our greatest competitor. We all are going to hit walls. It is just a matter of how early and how often. How you handle these moments is the difference that separates the good from the greats. You must go deep within yourself and face your fears to achieve your full potential.

When I was striving to be one of the top realtors in the nation, the issue was not what the others did or how I could do something different. I simply had to overcome my fears. I had enough skill and talent to get to the top, but I had to focus on what I was doing and not worry about what other people were doing.

Being complacent may come from being more of a "knower" rather than a "learner". Being vulnerable, throwing away your notes, and seeking to educate yourself may be the push towards growth.

Everything Is Perfect

I've said it before, and I'll say it again. No matter what happens, you must live life from this perspective. It sounds simplistic, but in my life, this has been a great mantra. It especially applies when things don't go your way.

Here is an example from my life I briefly touched on earlier. I was an owner of a real estate franchise, Keller Williams Realty, in Fort Collins, CO. My two partners and I had four offices and more than 250 agents working with us. On the surface, everything looked great. The company generated more than $1 million a year in income from more than $340 million in sales.

Then the market shifted, and we had to make some decisions that would impact the company going forward. When that happened, it became clear to me that my partners and I were not aligned with what we wanted or how we thought the company should be run. We came to a major crossroads in the business.

I told my partners that I wanted either a 51% controlling interest in the company, or I wanted out. However, instead of buying me out, my partners decided to sell our multi-million-dollar company out from under me. Together, their two-thirds majority interest outvoted me, and they could sell the company and all of our assets without my consent.

I still had choices. Fight and get into a long, expensive legal battle or leave and move on with my life, even though that choice would cost me hundreds of thousands of invested dollars as well as the potential to make millions over time. I cannot lie: I was angry—for about a week until I chose to move on and say that everything was perfect.

I thought I was partnering with two people with whom I was aligned on everything from morals to spiritual beliefs. When the market began to shift, they slid into a scarcity mindset and made poor decisions versus being in an abundant mindset that we could create something good out of the challenges we faced.

I could have sat down and cried about the money I lost and the future opportunities I lost because of these people. I could have beaten myself up, saying how stupid I was to not see that we were not aligned before I got into this deal, and become a victim.

Instead, I chose to be a warrior and push ahead. If you were to talk to my staff, you would find out that they were far more upset than I. They kept asking me why I was not angrier or why I hadn't sued to regain my interest. I replied that I was not in control of this life, and I knew that God had a plan for me, and that I was going to have to wait to see what that was.

While I was deeply hurt by my partners and others I trusted, I had to move on. Later, I learned how much of my time was being drained by this ownership opportunity. Because of the time I freed up without having ownership in the company, I was able to acquire more than one hundred default mortgages that we took from the bank's outstanding debt. That happened because I had extra time to do research.

I started an oil and gas venture and bought dozens of houses nationwide, which I would not have had the time to do if I still owned the Keller Williams' franchise. Nor would I have had the time to buy our manufacturing company a year later because I would have been dealing with so many other issues within the real estate company.

By saying everything was perfect and moving forward, I was able to be a warrior instead of a victim and experience much bigger, sustainable gifts than I could see at the time. If I had stayed angry, I would have spiraled downward into a scarcity mindset and possible depression. Coming out on the other side, I see what the true plan was and what a blessing it was by keeping that mantra.

People become so focused on their goals that they forget a lot of the other great things going on around them. I have difficulty saying that I want to be number one because I know that your whole being can become engulfed in a goal versus enjoying the many other great things that are in life. Instead, I say that I want to do the best I can without sacrificing my friends and family, my health, my integrity, or anything else that is important to me.

What if you lived your life from this space? If you miss your plane, it is perfect. Just keep the perspective of processions and what great things might be ahead for you. It takes time to adopt this mantra, but I can tell you it is very freeing. Instead of being angry, I just say everything is perfect and go back to whatever I was doing. I focus on joy and that expands instead of focusing on the negativity and allowing that to expand.

Financial Abundance

Financial abundance may be difficult to define. It is not a matter of how much money one may have but rather how the financial resources you have may affect your bottom line and allow you to invest in others. So do not stay complacent; share and give, and everything will be perfect.

CHAPTER SEVEN
BUSINESS ABUNDANCE

Although I am an entrepreneur, I am not saying that working for someone is better or worse than being self-employed. However, if you choose to work for someone else, you have to play by their rules and let their morals and values drive you. If your morals and values are aligned, there probably will not be tension. If they are not aligned, you will dread waking up in the morning to go to work. When you own your own business, you get to create your own context. If you don't like the context you set, it is your own fault and you can change it whenever you want.

The most common conversation I have with people centers upon the desire to be self-employed. He or she may say, "I have this great idea. I want to become an entrepreneur and start my own business, invent a new technology. But I have to make money to feed my family, and I don't know how to transition."

What they are really telling me is that they are afraid to take a leap of faith. As the scarcity mindset hammers away at them, they can literally become paralyzed with fear.

The way to defeat fear in a new business idea is to break down the process into manageable steps and move through each one as if you were climbing a ladder. It is like the old adage: how do you eat an elephant? One bite at a time. Eating the whole thing is a daunting

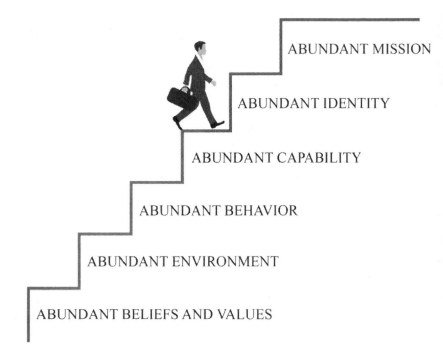

ABUNDANT MISSION

ABUNDANT IDENTITY

ABUNDANT CAPABILITY

ABUNDANT BEHAVIOR

ABUNDANT ENVIRONMENT

ABUNDANT BELIEFS AND VALUES

task, so people get scared and don't start. If you can build the business in small chunks, you are setting yourself up for success.

As you contemplate each rung of the ladder, think about where your strengths are and where you might need to learn more or get professional help if you lack clarity. Everything is adjustable, so do not be afraid to tweak the process as you go. As you climb the ladder, each rung builds on the others, and the whole process will take time and effort until you feel satisfied.

The way to defeat fear in a new business idea is to break down the process into manageable steps and move through each one as if you were climbing a ladder. It is like the old adage: how do you eat an elephant? One bite at a time. Eating the whole thing is a daunting task, so people get scared and don't start. If you can build the business in small chunks, you are setting yourself up for success.

It is important to remember that this is an evolving process. I encourage you to make changes and give yourself time to adapt within the space until you are satisfied with the results. At the same time, keep moving forward. You do not want to tweak your environment for a year before you get started. You also do not want to set an unrealistic timeframe in which you must have everything up and running.

Abundant Beliefs and Values

Values drive everything, and if you aren't clear on your values and beliefs, the rest doesn't matter. You need to get clear with your values before you start.

My values drive every decision I make. Am I going to have abundant values or scarcity values? Am I going to treat someone well because my values are similar to the Golden Rule? I think everyone should be treated equally and properly. Someone else's value system might not be based that way, and that will impact every aspect of their business.

I cannot stress enough that our values drive everything from whom we hire to what we do to what products we sell. And even what products we are not going to sell.

In Colorado, we have legal marijuana. Although it is legal, my personal values are such that I don't care if people want to use it, but I don't want to ever be on the news because some kid took edibles that I had a part in selling. So my values lead me not to participate in that business, regardless of how lucrative it may be.

I could have made good money on marijuana edibles and alcohol sales, but I turned them both down because they do not align with my values. I drink alcohol in social settings, which is different than selling liquor based on my values. I can have a beer, and that's different than me selling beer because I can control what I am doing, but I cannot control what others do. I think of it this way. If you try to drive home drunk and kill someone, I may not have forced you to drink, but I gave you the medium to make that happen. I have friends that have both businesses, which is fine. They just aren't for me and my family. When I look at a business I am considering starting, I ask myself, "Would I be proud to turn this over to my daughters?" I would be proud turning over a manufacturing company or real estate investments. But I don't think I would be proud to give my daughters a marijuana or liquor store.

If you are not clear about your values, nothing else matters. Some abundant values are integrity, love, and generosity. Some scarcity values are lying, deceit, cheating, and hatred.

Through life experiences, these values may become skewed. For example, someone may have a view that others are not equal to their standing. They look at who should get behind them in a line and why they should go first. All their decisions are made through that set of lenses instead of the abundant value of love which values everyone equally.

These morals and ideals are also called core values. They are the fundamental beliefs and guiding principles that dictate our behavior and action. Your core values will also be the values of your business and help to determine whether you are on the right path and fulfilling your business intentions.

Here are some values I helped to develop for a company named Burklyn to help get your thoughts going.

Burklyn Values: G.I.R.L.

Generosity: *Giving more than is usual or expected without anticipating anything in return.*

- Sharing is having more;
- Giver's get

Integrity: B*eing truthful and authentic in acts and statements regardless of consequences.*

- Respectfully tell your truth in every situation; "agree to disagree" is the minimum level of behavior.
- If any action or statement appears inconsistent with what seems proper to you, communicate your perspective to someone who can do something about it.
- Speak with good purpose; if it does not serve, do not say it. (Rolling Thunder)
- Listen with respect and with the intent to understand.
- When you disagree, or do not understand, ask clarifying questions. (Ben Franklin)
- Make only agreements that you are willing and intend to keep.
- If you cannot keep an agreement, communicate it as soon as practical to the appropriate person.
- Unless communicated in advance, return all communications (phone calls and emails) within 48 hours.
- When something is not working, look to the process for correction and propose a process-based solution.

Responsibility: *Devoting time and attention to the betterment of the planet.*

Above the line actions (inconsistent with the above)

- Act from the space: *"Communication is the response I get"*.
- Own the space: *I make a difference.*
- Agree that: *All my acts speak.*
- No matter what happens, look at the event from the context "It's perfect"

Love: *The unselfish and benevolent concern for the good of another.*

- Act from the space that *"Love is metaphysical gravity"* (Bucky)
- Seek the highest and best for all earthians.

- Be willing to understand and feel the emotions of others (empathy).

Below the line actions
- Laying Blame
- Justifying
- Shame

Being clear on your beliefs and values helps align you with others. This may help diminish encounters with conflict and allow for fuller relationships.

Abundant Environment

The environment you create lays the foundation for inspiration. The environment is the where and when. Where will you work? When can you devote uninterrupted time to your business? As with everything else, your environment begins with your mindset.

Designate a place or a room you can use as your home office. Is your work space or desk organized? Keep it free of clutter and non-business materials.

Unless you are single, if you work at home you will probably work around your family. I recommend you talk to your family members. Little things such as putting a sign on the door that says, "I am creating my business plan," or, "I am writing my book," can help to remind your family members you are working. Asking your spouse and/or your children not to disturb you unless there is an emergency reinforces the message that you are serious. You might set a timeframe of a few hours to work, and then take a break.

Renting a small office or suite might be right for you. That is also part of the investment for a bigger goal. I am more efficient outside of the home, so I have always had an offsite office. However, many people I know work better at home. You have to know which is better for you.

Think about times when you can work. Some people like the early morning before they go to their current job. I do my Bible studies early in the morning before the kids are up because I know that I have some leeway where I am not going to be interrupted. Some people work better at night. My wife loves to work at night. Some of my friends can stay up until three in the morning working on their businesses.

You might need total quiet or music in the background. Maybe you think better outside or at least near a window you can open. Think about the lighting in your space. Before you start, you need to know yourself to understand which environment is going to be best for you and which time will be most productive. If you haven't had to think about some of these things because they have been provided for you, then do some experimenting to find the best fit.

Abundant Behavior

Be very conscious of the behaviors you put into practice because you are forming habits that will drive your business up or down. When you create positive work habits, you can also create positive life habits that will generate abundant behaviors.

Turn off your email and your phone. Establishing the right behaviors takes focus, and you cannot focus when you are checking email and texting every five minutes.

Using a checklist might help you get into the habit of removing distractions and being prepared to work once you sit down. *Do I have my coffee?* Yes. *Is my email turned off?* Yes. *Pens, paper, computer?* Whatever you need to do your work. Most important, ask yourself, *What is my intention for today?*

The items on a checklist will be different for everyone. An author's behaviors are going to be different than someone who is trying to design a new product or someone who is trying to develop a business.

The author may need total silence. The product inventor might use their production time to talk to other people. The business developer might be out trying to raise capital.

Setting boundaries at the beginning is crucial. The behavior step lays the groundwork for realizing your direction and beginning to devise a plan.

Abundant Capability

Knowing your capabilities helps to define how you can chunk down your timeline into manageable parts. Always start with the big picture and work backward. The year intention creates tasks for your quarterly intention. By focusing on small, attainable intention, you will not get frightened because you are not trying to look at the end result from your emotional airplane. When I say an emotional airplane, I am just talking about a high level, 30,000-foot view where you can see all the parts.

Capability is also planning your strategy and determining how you will execute it. Preparing a timeline of action items, a strategy, and a plan will give you some key metrics by which you can measure progress and hold yourself accountable.

Understanding your strengths and weaknesses is very important. My strengths are the ability to conceive a bigger vision and formulate business ideas and strategy. My weakness is attending to details, such as day-to-day compliance and paperwork, which is why I have staff or other people who help me in those areas.

Of course, if you are just starting out or are a one-person business, you aren't going to have a staff. You might consider using a virtual assistant. Or you may want to hire a coach to help bring your weakness up from a D to a B even though it will still not become a strength. You may also ask a friend to help you in the beginning.

However, you should not attempt to do tasks where you may be weak. If you do, two things will happen: 1) you will get tired and frustrated because it is either work you dislike, not a strength, and may take you three times as long to produce anything; 2) you are probably not going to have the time to devote to producing a product with which you can be satisfied.

At this rung of the ladder, you could bring in someone to hold you accountable to keep your strategy in place and massage it as necessary. Brainstorming with others creates the diversity to help you see your blind spots and work through them.

The scarcity mindset will refuse to ask for help. Some people think that if they work alone, they should be able to do everything alone. They might also be afraid of failing before they even start so they do not want to hire the bookkeeper or coach to help them build a solid foundation.

The scarcity mindset will tell you to not only do everything yourself, but to keep all of your business to yourself. Let's say that someone starts a company and they know someone who is brilliant at technology. Although the expert could most likely help to get the enterprise on its feet faster, the owner does not want to give up any potential equity by inviting him or her to join the business. Although it is not about money because the company is nothing at this point, the owner is starting out with a scarcity mindset.

He or she would rather have 100% of something that is non-existent or mediocre versus 80% of something that can be amazing because they gave up some equity to another person.

As an example, I am in the process of developing a new app for the rental industry. I could have kept the entire project for myself, as it is 100% my idea, and I also have the capital to launch it.

However, I brought in a former AOL executive, who is not only brilliant but is an expert at analyzing start-ups and helping them to launch.

Although I will give up some equity, this project is going to be far better with his contribution. I believe the result will be three times more valuable because of this diversity. I like to say in a partnership 1+1 should equal 3. He has different contacts than I have in the tech arena, which has already added huge value.

Many of the people I see are on a rollercoaster curve instead of a steady incline. They try to do it all but get overwhelmed because as they get new clients, the paperwork and daily minutia increases. You must leave some empty space so that you have time to think and plan.

They are not making their calls, which drives production, so the next month is slow because they were too busy with the details to created new business. That cycle continues because they are working *in* their business instead of *on* their business.

Everyone has strengths and weaknesses. The better you can identify yours and get help where you need it, the better your chances are to create a successful business.

Abundant Identity

Who am I? That can be a daunting question. Your identity is what feeds your mission, that part of you that says, "I want to be part of something bigger." Your personal history is a huge part of your identity. Where you grew up, how you were raised and the influence of your parents and family are all factors in molding your identity.

Our self-concept is what we believe to be true about ourselves. Is it limiting or self-defeating? Your self-concept and self-esteem can determine your trajectory in life, and the sooner you pay attention to them, the more you can positively impact yourself and others. People starting their careers typically focus on financial gain, and people who are financially successful move beyond that and think about what kind of legacy they want to leave behind. At that point, they know that legacy is eternal. People with a high level of success understand that money can be gained and lost, but you'll more than likely not lose your legacy in the stock market.

Abundant Mission

Creating a mission statement keeps you focused on your goal. It is your elevator speech that tells the world what you are doing and why you are doing it. The mission statement ties into your beliefs and values.

A mission statement is a key tool that can be as important as your business plan. In it, you capture in a few succinct sentences the essence of your business goals and the philosophies underlying them. Equally important, the mission statement signals what your business is all about to your customers, employees, suppliers, and the community.

Knowing your why is helpful in this process. What drives you to create this product/service? Why do you want to help people? Two of the most important days in your life are the day you were born and the day you find out why you were born.

Being clear about your *why* is what I call putting logs on the fire and making that flame burn hotter so that you are driving harder towards your intention. If I offered you $20 to walk across a board on the ground, you would probably do it right away. If I suspended that same board between two windows on a high rise and offered you $20 to walk it, you would probably say no. Now if I offered you no money but your child was stuck on the other side and was in danger, you would walk across the board without hesitation. The difference isn't the money; it is the motivation driving you. When you find your why, you will be motivated not by money but by something burning deeper inside of you.

Apple and HP both make computers. Apple's *why* is wanting to challenge the status quo and be different. HP's *why* is wanting a faster computer. I think this difference is what has catapulted Apple past HP.

A company called *Know Your Why* tells us, "The WHY is about providing you with clarity, which allows passion to manifest and in turn becomes inspiration—the inspiration to improve all aspects of your own life, inspire those around you, and make the world a better place."

In his book *Start with Why*, Simon Sinek describes *why* as "the purpose, cause, or belief that inspires you to do what you do".

If you're like I was, you probably think there are a million *whys* that motivate people. Sinek believes there are only nine known whys on the planet. Many start at a high level, but once they drill down you should arrive at one of the nine *whys* below.

- To do it the right way
- To simplify things
- To find a better way and share it
- To create clarity
- To make sense of the complicated and challenging
- To contribute to a greater cause
- To be trusted/trustworthy
- To seek knowledge and understanding
- To challenge the status quo and think differently

However, only one is our core *why*, which is instilled in us at an early age. I have talked to a number of professionals, and they all say that your *why* doesn't change from childhood. It is so deeply encoded in your DNA that you will have the same *why* for life.

My *why* is do everything the right way. This concept drives me to keep experimenting with businesses and trying to put the right systems and processes in place. Inefficiency literally drives me crazy. I could be in a line at Subway watching the sandwich makers and see how they could tweak the team's workflow to get the most optimal return. This sometimes causes conflict with my wife and me, as I am always trying to change things. Sometimes it seems like I don't value her ideas. Being aware of what I am doing allows me to step back and look at any situation from her viewpoint.

Even though they may sound similar, the *whys* do not overlap. One will be stronger in you than the others, and this is your deepest value. I believe that if you ask a person what his or her *why* is, they answer with a *how* instead. For instance, they would say, "So I can provide for my family, be financially secure, etc." There are thousands of *hows*, but beneath all of those is one, deep-seated *why*.

How you execute your *why* should align with your beliefs and values. Think abundantly. Am I providing value for those around me? Am I bettering the world? Helping? Serving others?

The Triple Bottom Line

Most people only talk about the bottom line, the profit. The triple bottom line is people, profits, and planet. Have you looked at the other two Ps of the triple bottom line? How are you positively impacting the people that work around you and for you? By doing business with you, is their life better? Have you given any consideration to the planet? What are you doing to reduce your carbon footprint? Are you recycling at your office or buying recycled products to use?

Sometimes we get so caught up on the profit that we lose sight of these other important factors. Paying attention to the triple bottom line helps to build a strong company culture that will positively impact your profit.

It is okay not to have all the answers. You can find someone who specializes in areas where you need help. If you do not have the money to pay a professional, investigate places where you can get dramatically reduced services. Consider hiring a freelancer to outsource some of these tasks you are not good at.

What is stopping you from taking the next step? Whom can you ask for help to achieve your wildest dreams?

Create an MVP, Minimum Viable Product. This will help you to launch your idea faster and get momentum going forward. Reid Hoffman, founder of LinkedIn, says, "If you aren't a little embarrassed with your initial product, you waited too long to launch it."

Part of the learning process is evaluating and getting feedback so you can make it better. If you get what I call analysis paralysis (when someone spends so much time planning and organizing that they miss the opportunity or talk themselves out of it), you will never get started, and someone else will start selling the product you have sitting on a shelf. With the MVP, you can start with what Doctor Deming called the PDSA cycle. Deming is best known for his work in Japan after WWII, particularly his work with the leaders of Japanese industry. That work began in August 1950, at the Hakone Convention Center in Tokyo when Deming delivered a speech on what he called "Statistical Product Quality Administration". Many in Japan credit Deming as the inspiration for what has become known as the Japanese post-war economic miracle of 1950 to 1960.

Japan rose from the ashes of war to start itself on the road to becoming the second largest economy in the world through processes founded on the ideas Deming taught. Deming made a significant contribution to Japan's reputation for innovative, high-quality products and for its economic power. He is regarded as having had more impact on Japanese manufacturing and business than any other individual not of Japanese heritage.

Deming's teachings and philosophy are clearly illustrated by examining the results they produced after they were adopted by Japanese industry, as the following example shows. Ford Motor Company was simultaneously manufacturing a car model with transmissions made in Japan and the United States. Soon after the car model was on the market, Ford customers were requesting the model with the Japanese transmission over the US-made transmission, and they were willing to wait for the Japanese model. As both transmissions were made to the same specifications, Ford engineers could not understand the customer preference for the model with Japanese transmission. Finally, Ford engineers decided to take apart the two different transmissions. The American-made car parts were all within specified tolerance levels. On the other hand, the Japanese car parts were virtually identical to each other, and much closer to the nominal values for the parts—e.g., if a part was supposed to be one foot long, plus or minus 1/8 of an inch—then the Japanese parts were all within 1/16 of an inch, less variation. This made the Japanese cars run more smoothly and customers experienced fewer problems.

The PDSA cycle below is a systematic series of steps for gaining valuable learning and knowledge through the continual improvement of a product or process, also known as the Deming Wheel.

The cycle begins with the *Plan* step. This involves identifying a goal or purpose and formulating a theory, defining success metrics, and putting a plan into action. These activities are followed by the *Do* step, in which the components of the plan are implemented such as making a product. Next comes the *Study* step, where the outcomes are monitored to test for validity of a plan for signs of progress and success or problems and areas for improvement. The *Act* step brings the cycle full circle, integrating learning generated by the entire process which can be used to adjust the goal, change methods, or even reformulate the theory altogether.

These four steps are repeated as part of a never-ending cycle of continued improvement.

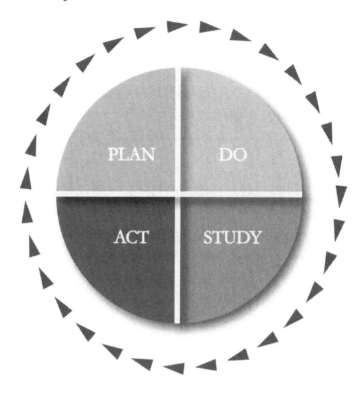

Let me give you an example from my life. When I started buying real estate, I obtained my real estate license in order to save commissions when I flipped the homes for a profit. That was my initial *Plan* step. Then I became a licensed realtor, the *Do* step. Next came the *Study* step, where I learned more about the market to determine what buyers really wanted and how I could do fix and flips. How I could help people buy houses took me to the *Act* step, where I deviated from my initial plan and started helping others learn how to buy and sell real estate.

Then I returned to the *Plan* step and looked for more great deals on houses, which lead me to start marketing to potential short-sale clients. Short sale is a process used to negotiate with mortgage holders. When homeowners become delinquent on their mortgage payment, the banks will usually take less than the amount remaining on the loan in order to sell the house as quickly as possible to avoid foreclosure.

After that, I was back to the *Do* step and marketing to sellers that were behind on their mortgage. At the peak, I had about 100 short sale listings, which was the top in Northern Colorado. I then moved to the *Study* step, noticing that short sales were getting rejected and taking longer to get approved because the banks didn't have a good system to process the number of requests they were getting. This meant we were going to see a lot of foreclosures coming out because banks couldn't work them out before the foreclosure sale. So I moved to the *Act* step and started to market to banks to list the foreclosures they were going to be having in the near future.

You see how this works? Creating a network and revolving through the Deming Wheel concept will keep you moving forward. You will build networks that can help you reach top financial decision makers and other professionals who you can help and who will help you. This is an example of 'sharing is having more'. If you are trying to build a business, I recommend that you find a way to do something similar. While there are thousands of marketing approaches, I think using a network and being willing to share is the fastest way to get to your intentions.

The triple bottom line: people, profit, planet. Keeping that in mind will help you to have a more sustainable and balanced business.

Staying in Motion

Not long ago, I met an anesthesiologist who had wanted to become a health and wellness life coach for more than 10 years.

As most people do, she was trying to figure out how to achieve her goal. She was afraid and unclear of the path to take that would lead to success.

"What does that look like in your future?" I asked.

"I don't know," she replied. Then, she closed her eyes and said, "It's foggy. I don't really understand how to get there."

"Great," I said. "Let's chunk it down."

Although we were strangers, I knew that because she was an anesthesiologist, she was most likely very by-the-book, very procedural, and very system-based. Someone in that mindset needs a road map with carefully planned destinations to help her reach her goal, which was health and wellness coaching.

As most people do, she was looking at a future that was a hundred miles away, and unless you're in an airplane, you cannot see that far. We need to gain some altitude to get a clearer perspective.

"Let's talk about focusing on just one coaching module on health," I suggested. "Determine what that would look like and what kind of content it would contain. Think about how much time you would need to create a base model."

"I can do that," she said. "I can probably have some decent content built within 20 hours."

By breaking down the process into small, attainable intentions, we can shut down the noise in our heads. I need a business plan. How do I attract customers? Who is my customer?

All she needed was an MVP, minimum viable product, to start her on her journey. I asked her to name three modules that she could develop at home with little money. She did.

Next, I asked her to determine an honest amount of time that she thought she could devote to working on the modules. This was difficult, because in addition to her schedule at the hospital, she had her children's schedules, family, and other personal commitments.

I challenged her to look at her schedule of where there was time wasted to be captured to seek her dream.

"What if you could free up just two additional hours a week?"

She thought about the obstacles she needed to work through in order to reorganize her time and told me that she thought she could devote 10 hours a week to her MVP. She figured out how to free up more time by setting up a carpool with other parents for their children. Of course, there are many behaviors that she will need to change along the way, but this was a great start.

Most people have time they can use toward their dreams, but they don't use it. They watch TV or do something else that isn't productive. It is more comfortable to drink beer on the couch than to do something that will challenge them to face their anxiety and the fear. If they do not start, they do not have to worry about failing. Just remember, if the action doesn't serve you, don't do it!

Next, I asked her where she would work on her business. I wanted to be sure she had a productive environment. I was hoping she wasn't working at the kitchen table where she was going to be interrupted. Anyone can put 10 hours aside, but after email and phone calls, they might get only one hour of work done. She had a home office where she thought she could be highly productive. Great. Check off the Environment box.

By brainstorming and asking her some thought-provoking questions, she was able to take the first step. She had thought of three low-cost modules she could work on to get started, and she had committed to 10 hours a week to develop them. We also talked about her skill set, and it was clear that she had the capability to execute the modules once she made time to focus on them. Capability box—check.

By taking one small, focused step, she could begin to create a positive forward motion. Once we get in motion, it is much harder to stop us. Getting going takes the effort. Remember, the rocket ship burns 96% of its fuel for takeoff.

Next, we talked about accountability. Being accountable to another person helps you stay in motion. Our anesthesiologist had two friends who agreed to call her every Friday for a progress report.

I asked her about meetup groups in her area. "Are there any groups or clubs in your area that meet about health and wellness?" I like to call the meet up groups 'test mice'. Meetup groups are great for testing your ideas and/or products. Having a group of people that are interested in the same field as you can give you great feedback. The best part about these groups is that most of them are free. Their responses will help you to work through problems before you go on Broadway and start charging money.

"Do you have groups of people that you can test this module on?" I asked.

"Yes," she said. "I belong to a meetup group with around 140 members." "Great. I am sure those people would be honored to be your test mice group and try whatever you build for your first module."

As with most of us, she had a fear of failure. We talked about her duties as an anesthesiologist, and how she must have also been fearful the first time she had to perform a spinal injection on a patient. However, the more procedures she did, the more her fear abated and her confidence grew. She went through the process and stayed in motion.

We also talked about giving herself permission to change course. She was clear about her mission to help people get healthy and achieve their personal goals, so we checked off that box. She had very strong values and an amazing work ethic, which made it easy to check off those boxes as well.

"I encourage you to try this for 30 days while keeping the security of your job," I said. "During that time, one of two things will happen. You may put another log on the fire and ignite a flame in you that makes you spend 25 hours a week on this project and work until two a.m. Or, after trying on this metaphorical shirt, you might decide that you don't like the way it feels, and this isn't where you need to go. If that happens, you hang the shirt back on the rack, and tell yourself that everything is perfect and shop for another better fitting shirt."

Checking off the Identity box took a little longer. She struggled with changing careers from an anesthesiologist to a life coach. Suggesting that she try it first before making a final decision lessened the pressure of redefining her life. If she discovered that life coaching was not for her, nothing had changed. However, if she never tried, she would probably always wonder what could have happened had she taken a risk on herself. The freedom of giving herself permission to change course reduced the fear of failure.

I believe that she will throw another log on that fire, and then she is going to throw a tree on the fire, and it is going to burn so hot she will not be able to turn it off. Then, she will be on her way to a thriving coaching and mentoring career.

Changing your life is a huge step. Fear is a natural emotion. When you bring the focus close and reduce the project to a progression of manageable steps, you remove the fear and stay in motion.

Time Is Irrelevant

Another obstacle to staying in motion is age. I see it all the time. You may tell yourself that you are getting older and only have one shot to achieve your goal. If you don't do it now, you never will. Again, you are trying to see a hundred miles ahead.

All you need to do is put one foot in front of the other and start climbing up the ladder. Each step you climb allows you to see farther down the road. Soon, you will be able to see your goal and realize your vision.

The Sober Second Thought

When we get so caught up in the situation and are so busy being busy or being fearful or laying blame or beating ourselves up, we never stop to think about what we are doing or where we are headed. That's when it's time to hit the pause button.

When we are so caught up in the to-do, we forget to dream and let our mind wander. Once, when I was in the middle of an intense situation, one of my mentors, Marshall Thurber, encouraged me to go find a park bench. While it didn't make sense to me at the time, his advice has proven to be a great gift in my life. He calls it a sober second thought. Taking quiet time allows you the space to pull back from a situation that you are too close to so that you can look for better solutions.

Even taking a sober second thought before sending an e-mail can save problems. I have sent e-mails that I wish I could get back. If I had taken a minute to go for a walk or slept on it and then reread it before sending, I might have felt differently and saved myself and the recipient grief. Maybe I could have had someone else read it and get their feedback instead of replying while my tension was high. We try to be so laser-focused that sometimes we forget that procrastination can be very fruitful.

One of my favorite ways to accomplish this is by mind mapping. One of my favorite books on this subject is *Mindmapping: Your Personal Guide to Exploring Creativity and Problem-Solving* by Joyce Wycoff. The book shows how to use images, words, phrases, or whatever comes to your mind which helps improve brainstorming and collaboration sessions.

The sober second thought is useful to stop and evaluate before making a decision, especially during big decisions. Make a conscious decision to take the time for that sober second thought.

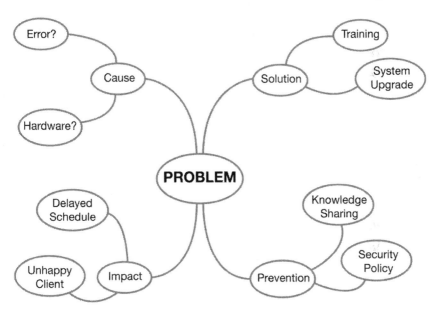

Know When to Fold 'Em

Knowing when to quit is one of the hidden gems that lead to success. When I was 20, my goal was to work for Sysco Foodservices, a Fortune 500 corporation. To me, it was a fantastic company where I could make great money and talk about food, which I was very passionate about.

At the time, I was an executive chef. I started out as a dishwasher in a small greasy-spoon restaurant. When I finished with the dishes, I would get on the prep line to learn how to cook. Before long, I was a full-time cook and after working in two more restaurants, found myself in the kitchen of one of the largest banquet facilities north of Denver. I worked my way up to executive chef in charge of the staff and kitchen, which was an interesting experience. Most of the people, including the dishwashers were 10 to 20 years older than I, and a handful of them were 30 to 40 years older.

One of my duties was to interact with the sales rep from Sysco Foods who came in to sell us groceries and other industry items. Eventually, I told him that I was tired of working nights and weekends. I was never around to celebrate holidays like Valentine's Day with Lindsay, my high school sweetheart, or Mother's Day with my mom. I told him I was looking for a job with more flexibility.

Thanks to my sales rep, I got an interview with Sysco and was offered a position as a marketing associate. To my knowledge, I was the youngest person ever hired as a marketing associate in Sysco history. Even at 20, I had an in-depth knowledge of the food industry, which was of very high value for them. They also thought I was highly driven, had the right personality, and already had knowledge of their products. Again, I was the youngest guy in the room. Most of the sales associates were between 40 and 50 years old.

In many large corporations, there are incentives, such as major trips, to boost sales. During the five years I worked for Sysco, I won 13 of the 16 promotional awards. My sweetheart became my wife, and she and I enjoyed all-inclusive trips to places like Hawaii, Georgia, Key West, California, and a number of other amazing destinations. We also had other promotions like gifts and cash prices.

Everyone had the same rules. Everyone knew the business. Most of the other marketing associates had been in the business much longer than I. So why was I so successful? Because I was willing to take time to learn the rules. Some of the reps wouldn't take samples of new products to give to the customers. Some didn't want to spend extra time building their client lists. They weren't willing to go out and hustle our promotional items. Our performance was based on the amount of the promotional products we sold the previous year and the increases we sold in the current year. My success was nothing more than knowing how to play the game and playing as hard as I could. However, I always followed the rules and operated in integrity by never selling a customer something he or she did not need just to win a prize.

For me, building systems and following them to achieve my goals is very satisfying. As everything is very system-generated for me, I figured out a way to work between 20 and 25 hours a week doing the same job that others spent 50 to 60 hours doing. In that business, there are high-need, high-touch clients and low-need, low-touch clients. Low-touch customers are the ones that pay on time, have one or two large orders per week instead of three or four small orders, and have enough cash on hand to order an extra box of hamburgers so they don't run out. Small, start-up restaurants usually do not have much extra money. They order just enough to replenish their stock and frequently end up ordering several times a week. I began to focus on larger customers and spent a lot of time fostering those relationships.

I began to constantly purge my accounts and give my high-maintenance clients to new reps who were just starting in the business. I would say, "Here are three accounts to cut your teeth on." While I lost a little money because of the commission-driven job, I gained the time to go after one more high value customer that ended up being more profitable than the three I gave away. The new associate was happy to have the clients because he or she was building their client base and had the time to service these high-maintenance customers while they learned the business. That process freed enough time for me to start flipping houses, research my current market, and start investing, which became my true passion.

Having two careers also brought me to a crossroads. One day my regional manager called me into her office. She said that she thought that real estate was taking too much of my time. She didn't believe I was fully committed to Sysco. Then she told me that I had to make a decision.

"We know you're only working part time," she said. "And we want you to be committed to work fulltime for Sysco. You have the choice. Either work for Sysco fulltime, or turn in your computer. You can't have it both ways."

"I don't understand," I replied. "I'm hitting all my numbers, and all of my collections are current."

"I agree. But I know that if you focused on Sysco full-time, you could do great things. We just really need you to be committed to your current role."

As a team leader, my manager's bonuses depended on how well her team performed. If I produced more, I could help offset others who weren't performing as well, and then she would make her bonus.

Initially, my intention had been to work for Sysco because it was a Fortune 500 company where I could make great money and have a secure future. However, by being abundant, I had the choice to either stay at Sysco or pursue my dream of real estate investing. I chose to take a risk on myself and leave.

I told my boss, "I'm sorry you are forcing me to make a choice, but I'm afraid I can't commit to Sysco full time."

You could see the surprised look on her face because I was one of her top performers. I think she thought that I would give up my real estate side business and fully commit to Sysco. She knew I was making six figures and most people wouldn't walk away from such an opportunity. Instead, I stood, offered my hand, and thanked her for being a good manager.

While it may be a difficult decision to make, there comes a time when you need to be clear with your goals and align yourself with opportunities to achieve them. Best to know when to hold 'em and when to fold 'em.

New Options

One of the common questions I get is how did I get started in buying real estate. When I was about fifteen years old, I read *Rich Dad, Poor Dad,* the Robert Kiyosaki book on investing, and realized that if I wanted to make money work for me instead of me working for money, I had to do more than just put it in a retirement account and hope there would be enough to provide for me and my family in the future.

In the book, he talks about living from paycheck to paycheck, which really inspired me because of the financial difficulties my parents had suffered. He talks about how people will get a bonus and buy a boat. Or get a raise and create more bills to spend it. Many are trapped in the cycle of working for money instead of having money work for them. I think many people are constantly trying to keep up with the Joneses. They want what others have so they can fit in.

So I asked myself what I could do to get out of that cycle, and the only way I was aware of at that time was through real estate.

I'd been doing lots of research into buying real estate and was looking for an opportunity to invest when my girlfriend's aunt called her mom. Her aunt lived in another state and rented the home she was in for more than 10 years; she'd just learned that her elderly landlord needed to sell the home. She wanted to stay in the house and the neighborhood she had been in for so long but could not afford to buy the place.

I was excited at this great opportunity. I knew her aunt had kept the house in good condition. I told my girlfriend's mom that I wanted more info and that I would probably buy it. I gathered all the info and did my research. I ended up offering the owner market value for the home sight unseen. I thought once I owned it, my girlfriend's aunt could just keep renting the house from me.

My girlfriend's parents, who had been discussing the aunt's situation, questioned me about what I was contemplating.

"This house is in Texas, and we live in Colorado. Are you going to fly down and look at it? How do you expect to buy it sight unseen?" her dad asked.

"I don't need to see it. I can pay for an appraisal once I know what the value is. I can apply for a loan." I was still living with my parents so I really didn't have any bills.

I thought that as long as she could afford to pay the same amount of rent, I should be able to make a small profit. The house was $40,000, so I figured even if it was a total train wreck it wouldn't kill me. I put 10% down, which was $4,000, and got a loan for $36,000. My payments after taxes, principal, interest, and insurance was $417 per month. I was getting $600 in rent, so I would have a positive cash flow of about $183 per month. I thought this would allow me to learn about rentals without a huge risk because it was a lot cheaper than houses in Colorado averaging $200,000 at the time. The owner accepted my offer, and I was on my way to being a landlord. I was 18 when I closed on the house, and this was the first step in really learning about the industry.

I could see that her parents thought it was a crazy idea, and they strongly advised me not to buy the property. Her mother was very concerned that I was being reckless. I know she was just being protective because she cared about me, but I had to follow my heart. Even some of my friends thought I was crazy because I didn't know anything about buying real estate, especially buying and managing my first asset in another state. However, I chose to operate from the abundant mindset. When an opportunity appeared, I grabbed it.

At the time, the mortgage market was booming. If I could sign my name, I could get a loan, so it was much easier to buy houses than it is now. That's when I began to learn about leverage, of using the bank's money to earn money. I learned about how rental income would pay my mortgage while I gained equity in the property. I would also start to learn how I could write off interest, property taxes, and depreciate the house, which could save me money on my taxes. That first transaction had confirmed that I made the right choice getting into real estate, and it had been fun.

I don't believe I would have the investing success if I had played it safe and stayed in the corporate world working for Sysco. I took the risk and followed what I believed was the abundant path.

I think most people know when they should quit. They get that gut instinct, but they do not act. They live in the scarcity mindset of fear of losing a steady paycheck, benefits, a retirement plan, or a certain lifestyle. When you operate out of abundance, you attract more choices.

There are times when you should forge ahead. There are also times when you need to take that sober second to analyze the situation you are in and ask yourself whether or not you are where you are supposed to be and whether you're doing what you are supposed to do. Giving yourself permission to quit frees both your time and emotions so you can go after your true desires. You cannot be of service to yourself, your family, or others when you are continually running on empty. Having dyslexia has made me think outside of the box and into the future. Thinking abundantly does the same thing.

When you take time to analyze your emotions, you find opportunities that give you more choices in life. You take control. You gain experience so you know when to quit and when to rally and push through a tense time. Sure, you will strike out sometimes, but if you want to hit a homerun, you need to keep swinging that bat.

Develop Your Leverage

There are lots of forms of leverage: it can be time, talents, or financial leverage. In all of my businesses I have a lot of leverage which allows me to live abundantly, financially as well as with my family, creating abundant opportunities to help others.

In my real estate company, my office staff does all the paper-work, follow-up, compliance, agent communication, client communication, and other administrative duties, which allows me the time to grow the business. Sitting in my office all day doing paper-work would neither benefit me or the company. I'm not good at detail work or repetitive tasks. Being forced to do them would be frustrating, and I would not feel that my job was rewarding. Having someone handle administrative work who is good at it and enjoys it is a gift to both of us. Trying to do it all would also impact my family. I would not be able to be home at a decent hour during the week or spend the weekends with them.

I have a sales team that focuses solely on our buyers. Helping a buyer find the right home or investment property takes the bulk of any realtor's time. Having a dedicated team allows me to help more people, and as they do the lion's share of the work, I split my commission 50-50 when escrow closes. This is a win-win scenario because I give them the abundant extra leads in my life, they get extra business they would not have had, and I get more business that I would not have had time to handle.

In our oil and gas company, the initial investment is time and research. Once you have the projects running, you can let the oil pump go up and down and have the operator monitor them on a daily or weekly basis. Aside from a handful of decisions that have to be made, you can make money without having to do hours of work.

On the lending side, we act like the bank and perform the due diligence at the beginning of the loan and then collect payments.

We only have issues if someone doesn't pay, but typically our loan-to-value is very favorable so we would get back a house with far more equity than we lent which makes the extra work worth the while.

In our real estate portfolio, most of our assets are managed by local management companies. Once a month, we balance the books and manage repair requests. Having the management company attend to these issues relieves me from receiving calls Christmas night saying a toilet is leaking or the heating system isn't working. This is an invaluable service. And the people who rent my houses pay my mortgages and increase the value of my assets, which is another degree of financial leverage.

In the manufacturing company, we have staff to handle the bookkeeping, assembly, order processing, shipping, and other day-to-day operations. Our suppliers contribute as technical experts or have special-equipment resources that help us complete the job faster. I am not interested in any business without high leverage. When I look at a new idea, I always look at the leverage. How much money will it take to get X return? And how much time will the new venture require? At this season of life with young kids, time is a huge value to me. So if a business is going to require a lot of my time, I would probably say no to the new venture.

Financial leverage can be very powerful, but you must use discretion. Many people that have gotten rich from using leverage, and many have lost everything. I know several that got high loan to value loans with little or nothing down. The market shifted a little bit, and they were over-leveraged and lost everything because they couldn't sell. Or numerous like me had rates adjust and had so many negative assets that it took them down.

I had an opportunity to spend some time with a billionaire heavily invested in real estate. I asked him, "When do you know that you are using too much leverage?" His answer was simple.

"When you can't sleep at night, you know you're over-leveraged."

Warren Buffett says you should not test the depths of a river with both feet, meaning that you should enter the leverage field cautiously. Instead of jumping, go slow and learn everything you can so that you do not end up over your head.

Leadership Abundance

"People don't buy what you do; they buy why you do it. And what you do simply proves what you believe." — Simon Sinek, *Start with Why: How Great Leaders Inspire Everyone to Take Action*

Founders Create Vision and Hand Off to the Specialists

We wouldn't tell our friends not to do what they are not good at, but every day people everywhere do tasks that they should delegate to someone else. Delegation is one of the traits of great leaders. They delegate the tasks they should not be doing.

As I have said, I am terrible at paperwork and administrative tasks. I have a great team to do these tasks, so I can focus on the lifeblood of my business. I joke in my business that I have the tendency to throw grenades over my shoulder. I love to create and do new things, and then I throw it over my shoulder for my team to sort out the details and execute.

Good leaders also have a mission and vision statement for the company. If you do not know where you are going, it will be hard to recruit a team who wants to follow you. You must be clear about your values so that you attract like-minded people and then put those people to work. You may consider what might be the "best fit" for your needs and what type of talent you desire. A simple way of thinking about it is a bunch of people in a boat paddling. If they paddle in the same direction, it is an easy journey. If everyone paddles in a direction they think is good, they will just spin in circles.

Hire Top Talent

Never settle for a warm body because you need the help.

A friend of mine has a business that has constant staff turnover because she shortcuts the hiring process. She's always short-staffed because she hires the first person who can fog a mirror, only to later discover that the person was not a good fit or did not have the skills the job required. Because she is kind and reluctant to let someone go, she keeps the substandard employee around hoping they will improve or change their personality.

To avoid this pitfall, make a list of non-negotiable traits and do not hire the candidate unless you can tick all those boxes, including having the same moral values. When you consider how important hiring people with the same values is in your business, you can save yourself months of training on this one point alone. Hiring someone who is already aligned with your values eliminates the time and effort of trying to teach them all those standards such as being on time, being generous, striving for win-win solutions, and sharing.

One of my friends, who has an amazing special needs son, formed a business partnership with someone who called people retarded if they were slow on the job or did not understand things. If my friend had been clear with her moral values at the beginning, she would have never agreed to this partnership, knowing how much that word and the judgment it implies bothers her.

Instead, this misalignment of character will most likely cost her at least $100,000 as they work to split their business, not to mention the stress this has caused her. Trying to dissolve a business relationship is a tough example of what can happen when you do not take the time to discuss the factors that are most critical to you.

One thing I do when checking references is to ask the reference person for one additional person's name to call. This will give you another degree of separation from the happy references, the people the candidate knows who will give him or her a raving review. If the candidate gives you permission to contact his or her current employer, always ask whether they would rehire the candidate.

Now that you have found the right person who aligns with your mission and values, you must make sure you have the right person in the right seat. I think people find good people and just think they can put them anywhere. If you have the right person in the wrong seat, it will be an uphill battle for both parties. Also, you must ask the candidate questions about what they want and what an ideal job looks like.

The DISC Assessment

I like using an online tool called a DISC test. The DISC acronym stands for dominance, influence, steadiness, and conscientiousness. This reliable behavior assessment test has been used by more than 50 million people since it was first introduced in 1972.

Each leader should take the test themselves as well. This will help you validate roles you should be doing and roles you should be hiring for. The test can help you find people who have strengths you lack, and those are the ones you want on your team. For instance, I am almost 90% dominant and 8% influential. Steady and conscientious are nearly non-existent in my assessment. Therefore, my staff consists of people who scored high in those S and C areas. They are reliable, steady, and compliant. They make sure all the "I's" are dotted and the "T's" are crossed.

Another good friend of mine told me that she does not have time for the hiring process. I asked her why she was still doing the hiring instead of finding one person who is clear on the company's values and mission and letting them hire and train new staff. Filling your company with the right people is key to your success, and that begins with one key hire. Once you hire and train the top talent, they should be able to take over the hiring and training process, and you can pass the baton.

Another simple but important question is to ask yourself whether or not you want to work with this person every day for maybe a long time. Trust your gut feeling. At the end of the day, hiring comes down to if it is not a clear yes, it should be a clear no.

One of my business partners and I have something we call the NAR, the No Asshole Rule. Everything from the interview to the DISC to the references may be outstanding. However, if you do not feel right about someone, do not waste your time. Life is too short to work with people you do not enjoy and trust. This rule applies to clients and vendors as well. Why do people let a client continue to abuse them? It makes no sense, as there are lots of clients out there. Don't be afraid to fire an abusive one and move on. Your day and week will go much better without them. When you go to your next appointment, you will perform better because you will come in with a positive attitude instead of being angry for what the bad client just said or did to you.

When you have the strongest possible team in place, it is your job to lead them to differentiate themselves from the competition. Do not hire people just to fill a position overall. Enroll them into your dream.

Abundant Business

This chapter discusses several ways in which one can strive for an abundant business. Whether it is identifying your "why", developing abundant behaviors/beliefs/values, or knowing when to "hold 'em or fold 'em", the main idea here is to start making strides towards evaluating your current strategies and determining whether they will help you create an abundant business.

CHAPTER EIGHT

ABUNDANCE OF TIME

Think you don't have enough time to learn anything new?

Brian Tracy, international best-selling author and inspirational speaker, recommends turning your car into a mobile classroom. Based on an average of 12,000 miles driven each year, you can gain two semesters of education just by using your driving time as a classroom.

Being dyslexic, I always have a hard time reading and still do not retain much of the information. Once audio books became popular, I started to like to "read" again, or in my case listen. I took what Brian said to heart and not only listened to books in my truck but also at the gym. The average audio book is about seven hours long; I can get through two books a week just by using my truck and gym time. It would be hard not to learn something within a year if you listened to 104 books, right?

Time management is nothing more than believing you have enough time in your day and your life to accomplish anything. Instead of telling yourself that you do not have time, look at the situation and ask yourself how you can optimize your time.

Let's look at a typical day in my life. First, I want to be clear that I am not trying to boast and say my way is the right way or the only way. I only want to demonstrate that I practice what I preach.

My Typical Day

My day starts around 6:30 a.m. so that I can have quiet time to read the Bible and spend time in prayer before my children are up at 7. I know my kids will be up around 7 a.m. because they have clocks that turn green at 7 when they can come out of their rooms. Our young kids were always early risers, so I would lose sleep and my quite time. I had to find a way to get some structure back in both of these areas, so these clocks have been great. I make breakfast for my two daughters and help my wife get them ready for the day. After that, I go to the gym at 8:30 a.m. I finish my workout, shower, and head to the office by 10 a.m.

Next, I work about two hours before lunch, which can take between one and two hours, depending upon whether or not I have a business lunch. Then I go back to the office and work until 5 p.m.

I spend evenings with my family and do not work nights or weekends. Even with all the businesses I am involved in, on average, I work about 30 hours a week total. By condensing my schedule, I must be disciplined when I am working. It is like when you waited to get your homework done at the last minute in school. You can always get it done faster than if you had weeks to work on it because you have a sense of urgency.

We need to focus our efforts on the 20% of our work that generates the desired results, even if we work for someone else. Many of us spend most of our days doing the 80% that does not help us achieve our goals—those mundane administrative tasks such as filing reports, paperwork, and answering emails.

This mindset doesn't just work for business owners. It worked for me when I worked for Sysco Food Services. Remember, I handed off the low-volume, high-maintenance accounts to new agents. The new agents gained more commission and clients, and I gained valuable time to expand my territory and increase my sales. I also used the extra time I gained to start building my Real Estate business.

Maybe in your job you are not trying to increase your sales. Maybe you are trying to free up time so that you can go to your child's basketball game. Or you just want to go home and relax to fill your tank with relationships or the hobbies you enjoy.

It all goes back to the age-old saying of work smarter, not harder. You can always streamline your work and your life. I remember when I worked 70-hour weeks. I would tell people with pride, "I am working a ton," like it was a good thing. Now, when my friends say they are working 70-hour weeks, I just say, "Wow. That sounds terrible." I think for men especially they feel that working a lot validates them. I love to challenge them with this eye-opening exercise.

Print out a spreadsheet with five-minute time blocks and record what you did during each time period. Keeping the cycle time short will help prevent lengthy explanations. Don't write a story; just jot down a quick couple of words such as email, phone call, worked on presentation, and so forth. [Maybe make a diagram or short display.]

No one's going to see this but you, so be honest. You will find out how much time you waste on non-business matters such as texting, email, and perusing the Internet or Facebook and other social media sites. Your spreadsheet will reveal exactly how much time you have to invest in your family, hobbies, or even a new venture, and how much time you waste. Although this exercise might sound like a waste of time too, I assure you that if you do it, it will be an eye-opening experience. After you complete the time-tracking exercise, ask yourself these three questions:

- Does this task require my expertise to accomplish?
- How much can I afford to pay someone else to do this task?

- Do I enjoy this task?

If you get to the point that you are truly productive all day, you need to find someone to help you or something to give up and add that leverage to your daily tasks. What tasks can you delegate? Where can you streamline your work? If you could remove one job today, what would it be?

Can you time-block emails so you are not stuck all day chasing answers? Can you set up rules in your email so that things get forwarded without you touching them? Could you use a virtual assistant for research or nominal tasks? When you need help, you should get it. You cannot build your business or help anyone else when your tank is empty.

Luckily for me, I had an impending event that forced me to analyze how I was using my time, tasks I was doing, and systems I had in place. My impending event was a mission trip to Cambodia. I was going to be on the Mekong River and off the grid for 14 days. I knew that all of my businesses were going to have to run without me for two weeks. This forced me to really see how strong the training of my team was and how strong my systems were. I started by looking at everything I was doing and had to figure out a way to have someone else do all these tasks for at least two weeks. I had to make sure my training was documented and they were proficient in the tasks. I started preparing almost two months in advance because for me this was my livelihood at stake.

I diligently trained my team then sat back, monitoring them do everything from A-Z. This is when the harsh reality set in for me that I was the weakest link on the team. They were getting things done better and faster than I got them done. They started to find other processes to integrate into our systems. I was the only thing slowing us down from growing to the next level. I needed to be focusing on growing the business and coming up with new ideas, not doing the day to day tasks. This was a huge aha moment in my life. A seemingly scary, impending event of being off the grid and out of communication for two weeks was one of the greatest gifts of my life. I was such a control freak, and I was holding onto every task instead of letting go and empowering others.

It is so great to put other people into your processes to see how well it is documented. When you give them the manual or procedure book, don't say anything; let them follow the written process for a given task. This will show you if you have your process documented well or what steps you are leaving out. Once you let one person execute the process, go back and revise the steps that you took for granted. So many people have office procedure books, but they are out dated or no one else has tried to execute the task. You should be able to sit anyone down and have them follow the step by step instructions if you do your documentation right. Stick with this and make sure all your processes are air tight. This will give you the comfort that things are being properly cared for if you are gone.

Don't get me wrong. While I was gone I still had a little anxiety about not knowing what was going on. I got home and everything was running perfectly. When I got back from my trip, I left 90% of my tasks on my team's plate, and I never looked back. I trusted my team to do what they do best so that I can focus on what I do best. By spending the time to check my systems, it allowed me to be free from a life of work bondage.

Is there a way that you can create an impending event to force you to outsource or delegate tasks you shouldn't be doing? This could be one of the greatest gifts you can give yourself. At least taking the time to say, "If I was gone for two weeks, who could do what, and are they trained to execute these tasks?" By taking this time, it will expose what you can get off your plate so you can do what you need to be doing. Now I can travel for multiple weeks and don't even need to check my cell phone, knowing it is all under control. People make fun of me because when I was a realtor my number wasn't listed anywhere. I learned that my team could answer 98% of the questions that people called me about. This drove some agents that wanted to talk to me crazy, but I was in control of my time, not them. Having a competent team allows me to not even take phone calls most of the time. They pass on the ones that need to be, but my phone probably rings only a couple times a day, which allows me to be focused.

People on their death beds often wish they could turn back the clock and attend their children's school programs or just sit home and cuddle on the couch, watching a movie. However, they were too busy at work. What action can you take today so when you are on your death bed, you can say you gave it your all and lived well?

Your focus this year should be to delegate as many non-vital functions as possible. Now, I get that it probably does not make sense to hire a driver to take you to an appointment. But maybe you can have the client come to your office, as I typically do. This saves so much time.

You are the rainmaker generating the business, so only do the vital rain-making tasks. Remember, there is a difference between vital tasks and vital priorities. Vital priorities are the things that people do to meet deadlines and push agendas forward.

There is no perfect balance, just a continuing counterbalance. As Albert Einstein said, "Life is like a bicycle. To keep balance, you must keep moving."

Take time to consider what elements in your day hinder your time and productivity. If you made changes to your day, how would this free up more time? What would you do with this extra time? Abundance of time comes from time management, appropriate delegation, and identifying priorities even on a daily basis.

CHAPTER NINE
ABUNDANT GIVING

I have been blessed to be able to take part in two mission trips with my local church, one to Honduras and one to Cambodia. Because we had abundance, we were able to go and share some of our time and money with people in need.

It is incredibly humbling to go on trips like this because you can see how much we take for granted as Americans. Those born in America won the lottery just by being born in this great nation. Even if you are poor in the U.S., you are still much richer than most people in the world. Some of the people we visited do not have a home. Many, who do live in "homes", have places that are barely habitable by American standards. These structures have broken roofs and dirt floors. Many consist of one large room, which includes the kitchen, only a stove in one corner of the room.

The space is mostly an open area where children do their homework if they are fortunate enough to go to school. At night, the room transforms into a collective bedroom where the family rolls their mats or spreads a blanket to create a barrier between them and the dirt. This house is maybe twelve-by-twelve feet square with five or six people living there.

Some, who are a little bit better off, have concrete houses with a couple of small rooms as well as a small kitchen area. The people we met subsisted primarily on a diet of rice. If they were lucky, they had fish paste to mix into the rice for flavor and more nourishment. Those who had a little more ate beans as well.

I remember being very conflicted when seeing those houses. I realized that my truck sleeps in a better place than most of these people. Think about that for a minute. My truck has a house. We just call it a garage in America. My truck's home has a solid roof, no leaks, is insulated so it is warm in the winter, windows that open and close, and even doors we can lock at night. I push a button, and the doors open by themselves. It was amazing for me just to sit there and consider that my vehicle sleeps in a better place than millions of people in the world.

For most Americans, that is normal. In fact, we want bigger garages so we can stuff them with more material things that will eventually all be thrown into a dump. When you pull into your garage tonight, just think about the fact that there are millions of people that are living in a worse place than our vehicles call home.

One of the great gifts of doing mission trips is getting to explore and learn about other cultures. When I was traveling, it was amazing to see how a six-year-old boy would be able to babysit his three-year-old brother. In our culture, it would be looked down upon and parents would probably get a visit from child protective services, maybe having their children taken away from them. But when you look at the cultures outside of America, this is a normal day. It makes me consider how capable children can be. They are more resilient than we realize, but in our culture, as we nurture them, we actually keep them babies instead of capable beings.

I remember vividly standing on a shoreline in Cambodia, watching these two little guys. The three-year-old boy fell and hit his head on a wood boat used for fishing. Yes, I said a boat. They were playing alone on the shore next to the Mekong River, the largest river in Cambodia and the twelfth largest river in the world. After the child hit his head on the boat, he simply stood up. That may not sound like much, but when you consider children in Western society who would cry and run to their mom, the difference was pretty amazing. I am not saying that it is not good to nurture children, but only that over-nurturing them builds a desire of needing help versus learning self-reliance and resilience that I think is so crucial to do great things.

Knowing some of these things has definitely served me as I have dealt with international clients. Understanding how these individuals were raised will really help in your interactions with them. The things that we take for granted or the way they act is probably not a byproduct of what they think of, but a byproduct of the environment they were raised in. What would happen if at a young age we started to empower our children to have more responsibility? I am not suggesting that we take away their childhood. I am simply saying that if we gave them more responsibility, they could build and grow into a self-reliant human that can make decisions and choices for themselves.

Now that I have been on these trips and taken some time to evaluate the impact we made, I am not as big a fan of most mission work as I once was. Although I think these trips are eye-openers and good for people like me, I do not believe they are necessarily a good idea for the local people. It is my pet peeve to not speak for others, so all I can do is talk about my experience. When I went on the mission trips, it changed something in me that I don't believe can be undone. It gave me such a heart and compassion for the people who could not help themselves, and I have vowed to make a difference.

In that regard, the trip was well worth it. Since then, we have supported helping people in these areas and are working on developing some projects that will benefit lives around the world. Without the exposure to the mission field, I do not believe I would have the burning desire to serve at the level I do today.

While we were in Cambodia doing vision and dental outreach, I saw that pulling a tooth that would eventually have fallen out probably is not going to change their lives. I witnessed a woman, who, after just having a tooth extracted, went out into the Mekong

River, one of the nastiest rivers I have ever seen in my life. She removed the cotton plug from the hole where her tooth had been and scooped up a handful of water to rinse her mouth. About 100 yards upstream, a farmer was bathing his cows in the water she was using. I wish I could better illustrate just how bad the water was. If we even stepped in the water, we washed our feet. We dared not drink this water, and we got sick even drinking the water that was supposedly cleaned for us.

If we had done what she did and put that water into our mouths, we would be hospitalized. Even from where we stood, we could see people washing their towels in the water and 10 feet away someone with a jug collecting water downstream.

In third world countries, you do not need a sophisticated license to practice medicine. Being someone who loves to experience new things I got to extract my first patients tooth as a dentist in Cambodia. We also did optical outreach, which was providing people two things. One was sunglasses and the other was vision correction glasses. The people needed sunglasses because so many of them work in rice fields; the reflection off the water from the sun as they bend over is very damaging to their eyes. Many of them also needed corrective glasses, just as we do getting older in America. Unfortunately, I was burdened with the task of picking who would come on the boat for the day's treatment. I had numbers and had to hand them out in the morning. I had to go out and look into the people's eyes to see if we could help them. Again, keep in mind, I am not a doctor, nor have I had any formal training in optometry.

Some had such advanced cataracts that glasses would not help them. They needed surgery. I would walk down the line of hundreds of people gathering hours before to pick 70 or 80 out of the crowd that we could possibly serve during the day. There was such need. We were on a large boat called the Ship of Life that traveled up and down the Mekong River to the rural villages that did not get much medical help and were too far from the city if they needed it. Most people did not have the money to get medical care, even if they could get to the city.

As we fitted our patients with glasses, it was fun to watch their faces light up. Speaking through an interpreter, one man told me that he did not know that there were leaves on trees. He thought it was just one big green blob. To be able to share his experience was very rewarding. I think a handful of the people will be able to use their glasses to better their lives and expand what they are able to do.

One woman, who used to weave baskets and sew, no longer had the vision to work. My hope is that having glasses will allow her to resume her sewing and basket-weaving so that she can make an income for her and her family. Unfortunately, I also saw what happened behind the scenes. Many of the elders basically have the right to take whatever they want from the younger generation. The elders are respected in these communities, so I watched young children give their glasses, customized for their eyes and their needs, to the older individuals. As we know, not all eyes are equal, so the glasses that work for one would probably not work for the others and neither person would benefit.

Another scenario concerns the people who work in construction, for example, and break their glasses. They have had good vision, for let's say six months, but do not have the funds to get their glasses repaired. So what I wrestle with now is whether we should let them live their life with poor vision or repair their glasses? Is it better to correct their vision and give them a short period of hope with the understanding that it may degrade or they may never receive another pair of glasses? Or let them go through life happy and oblivious to what 20/20 vision is?

While I think these types of mission trips help a few people, I really have to ask myself whether we actually moved the needle in this area. So many of these people could use technical skills or things that could actually move the needle and help them be sustainable. When I say move the needle, I mean have a lasting impact on them and the community. What are some of the other options of things that we could do to help serve people that have a more sustainable impact?

I am reminded of some things that Americans do. Our welfare system is one. There are situations where people get caught in vicious, generational cycles of staying in the system. We all know these cases and have seen people who know how to work the system to their benefit. What if we were able to offer them assistance to get them out of the system instead of enabling them to stay in the system? I think, in that context, mission work is very similar. If we could provide assistance and training that could actually allow people to earn an income for their family, we could make a generational impact where they could teach their kids and empower them in how to make money and have a good living.

For instance, let's say there were twelve of us on the trip to Cambodia, and assume the cost was $3,000 per person. What could we have done with $36,000 that would have had a more sustainable impact than we did? While I personally got value out of it, I was left wondering if there was a better way to help people. I love the book, *When Helping Hurts*, by Steve Corbett. It really brings these issues to light. As Americans, we always think that giving people things is the easiest way to solve their problem. I have found this is not the case in my travels to second and third world countries.

Organizations such as *Toms Shoes*, are trying to help people, but I have also seen how damaging it is in some of these countries. When *Toms Shoes* gives shoes to second world countries, they take business away from the person who owns the shoe store. Then the shoe store owner does not have money to go buy chickens from the chicken person. And the chicken person doesn't have money to go buy rice from the rice vendor. I think you can see how this could break down an eco-system. Some people don't have enough money to buy shoes from the shoe vendors, and some do. But just look at the ripple effect I have seen that it causes from a seemingly good deed. You also create the haves and the have nots.

Let's say *Toms Shoes* sends 100 pairs of shoes to rural Kenya. That's great for the 100 people who got shoes. But what about the 100,000 that did not? How do they feel? Let's say you have someone in rural Africa. They have lived their whole life just fine without shoes. Now you have introduced them to shoes, but you aren't always going to be there to keep them in shoes. *Toms* is not there to give them a replacement pair of shoes forever. This person has walked on their bare feet their entire life and was perfectly fine before they had their shoes. Now they have an experience of having shoes. They want and need new shoes, but they do not have the funds to replace them. Their feet aren't callused anymore because they have been softened in the new shoe.

I agree it is more comfortable to wear shoes than not, but what is the sustaining impact? Getting the shoes was not their idea. It was imposed on them by Americans operating on American standards. I am not trying to pick on *Toms Shoes*, just using them as one of many examples of when we try to help but it actually turns out that we could be hurting them. What would be worse? Never having shoes and living your life as you have. Or now knowing the difference of having shoes for a year, and then never getting another pair? Their feet have grown or they have worn them out; now what? What if we could give someone an opportunity to have a job so they can earn money to buy their own shoes this year, next year, 10 years from now and shoes for their children as well?

My desire is to find ways that companies like *Toms* with a giving heart can have a sustainable impact. This is my desire. Find a way that we can have a sustainable impact. I believe we should do this in America. I would rather pay for someone to get technical job skills that they could use to go out in the workforce instead of pay them to be on Medicaid for the next 30 to 50 years.

I understand that people fall on tough times and need help, but I think there is a vast difference from a generation who has been in the system for years and people in situational circumstances. Americans do things that ultimately leave people in worse positions, as I have seen through these mission trips. We go into these remote areas and build churches. We think it is great, and we feel good when we leave; but when we return to visit these areas, we see that the church is not being used. This also undermines people in the culture like men who feel like they should have provided that or built it.

Many times, it is abandoned because the local community does not take ownership of the church; they did not build it. In third-world countries, taking ownership of buildings is akin to owning a rental car. You do not own it, so you don't take responsibility for the maintenance. Have you ever washed your rental car before you returned it? Probably not. But you most likely wash your personal car on a regular basis because you own it.

If we gave them technical assistance and funds for materials, I think it would be a different scenario. A short-term mission is like a mouse dancing with an elephant. You might be good friends, but you may get stepped on and do more harm than good. We can't treat the symptom. We need to treat the disease. If someone can't pay their electric bill, giving money helps the symptom of needing money but not the disease of needing a job or building a budget.

If we focus on physical, we will focus on material things. If we focus on mental and spiritual, we can have sustained results.

We think that giving someone in a rural area a tractor would help increase production by 2,000%. To Westerners, this makes sense. However, we should get the feedback of the locals. Maybe a tractor isn't the best idea. Westerners want to McDonald's everything with what they think works for them. When you go to countries, you can see rusted equipment that didn't get used because they didn't know how to use it or how to fix it once it broke.

However, the McDonald's one-size-fits-all approach does not work most of the time. We must consider the people who become unemployed because the tractor is doing the work or that, when the tractor breaks down because a $.59 part failed, it can no longer be used. Nobody teaches the farmer how to maintain the tractor, so after a while, it sits rusting in the field.

One of the greatest things I have learned as I have traveled around the world is simply to ask better questions about what the peoples' needs are. Any time I have asked in second- and third-world countries what they need, the typical response is technical assistance or education. It is rare to hear people say they need more money. That is what we Westerners say. We think it is easier to give them money than find ways to mobilize technical teams to help people get better yield out of crops or trades so that they could go and earn an income.

You might be asking yourself, "If these methods aren't as effective, what are some options to have a more sustainable impact?" An organization I'm a board member for has brought about a new paradigm mind shift for me. Micro-financing is one of the most powerful ways I have seen to help people help themselves. Micro-finance is a general term used to describe financial services given to low income individuals or those who do not have access to typical banking services. Micro-financing is also the idea that low income individuals are capable of lifting themselves out of poverty by giving them access to financial services.

I am fortunate to be a board member of an organization called MCE Social Capital that gives micro loans in more than 30 countries. I have never seen higher leverage than this. The organization obtains a loan of let's say $500,000 from a bank in the United States. They then give that $500,000 to a local bank in, Ecuador for example. When I say a bank, it is not like Wells Fargo or Chase that we see on every corner.

Some are nicer, but most are more like gas stations. Keep in mind, these are second- and third-world countries. The local Ecuador bank then gives micro loans of amounts between $25 and $10,000. You can imagine the number of loans that could be made out of an initial loan of $500,000 to the local Ecuadorian bank. About 76% of MCE's loans are given to women because they have the highest repayment rate and are motivated by the need to feed their children. Our experience is that we had more defaults with men because they would buy alcohol or waste it on things that wouldn't increase the family's lifestyle. The locals are getting loans for a number of things such as buying a sewing machine or starting a new business to buy or sell goods in the market.

Some have medical needs and need a bridge loan. Other loan requests could be as simple as money to buy a refrigerator for their store so they can serve cold drinks instead of the warm ones they have been selling. The majority of these people live hand-to-mouth, meaning they have no margin in life: once the food is in their mouth they don't have extra. This is way worse than people that live paycheck to paycheck. Whether they eat or not can depend on if they made money that afternoon. These borrowers make payments back with interest to the local bank in Ecuador, and then the local bank in Ecuador makes one large payment to our organization or many others like ours. Our goal is to keep interest to the borrower as low as possible so we can just cover our costs. We are more concerned with making an impact than making a profit. There are other for-profit organizations where you can make a return on your money, but that isn't our desire at MCE.

I have been involved in a number of charities, and I have never seen leverage that has such a far reach or sustainable impact. The local bank teaches the borrowers about budgeting, which is a new concept in these second- and third-world countries. They teach them about saving by requiring a 10% reserve before they can get another loan. In some of the small villages, people borrow money as a group. For example, 10 women may borrow money collectively. They all are responsible for the other loans as well as theirs. They meet weekly to review the books and pay their proportional share of the interest for that week. The women not only get some adult time away from their businesses, but they also build strong bonds with other women trying to better their lives as well as their family's life.

When I was in Ecuador visiting some of the borrowers, one of my favorite visits was with a woman who needed money for a shrimp stand. I call her Mickey because she had a large Mickey Mouse tattoo on her chest. She buys shrimp from a local fisherman in bulk and sells it at the market to the locals. She borrowed the money to grow her business, and now not only is she providing for her family of four, but she has a couple of employees and is providing for their families as well. The best part of the visit was when Mickey said she has opened a second stand and her husband was running it. She smiled as she said, "He is working for me."

You don't know how rare this is in second and third-world countries. Women are sometimes treated like dogs. They have no value and are disposable, just there to bear and tend men's children. We were not only able to empower one woman to feed her family, but we are teaching her about finances so that she can pass knowledge on to her sons and daughters. She has become an empowered, strong woman whose husband works for her

One of the most interesting things about the micro loans is geo-political. The banks we do business with are not billion-dollar banks such as we have here. They may have $2 million to $5 million under management. It is typically easy to get money into third-world countries. It is very hard to get money back out because of the corruption and the fact that governments do not want the money to leave their country. Some charge up to 15% exit taxes to send the money back. Although we perform an analysis on each local micro-finance bank, the wild card is typically the geopolitical environment. Fortunately, we have a great team of people that manage this process.

A borrower in Venezuela was forecasting the national budget on $120 per barrel of oil. When we gave them a loan two years ago, everything looked good, and then oil went to $40 a barrel. Now 70% of Venezuela's domestic product has been depreciated almost 400%. As a result, their ability to repay their loans has been drastically altered, which is something we could not forecast. As we evaluate these loans, we must also look at the political environment. How much time is left on the term of the current government? Who is coming in? When is the next election? Are there any internal fights and battles like in many of the countries we avoid? All-in-all, it has been fun and very rewarding. I have been able to participate on our loan committee conference calls to approve various loans for MCE, which has been another great learning experience.

As a business decision, I always look for the highest leverage and how money can be used at the highest potential. So when I look at literally the millions and millions of people who we can specifically say are eating and having access to clean water and decent medical care through our loans, I believe there is no bigger impact. Most of us donate to some organization that does something good in the world. And yet, I have never seen an impact like micro-financing because of the sustainable results.

MCE (mcesocap.org) participates in other endeavors such as teaching health and wellness. Many of the people we serve do not understand calories and nutrition. If they are fortunate to eat a big meal, they are eating primarily carbohydrates, and then they sit around all day because it is hot. They do not understand about exercise or moving around, and so the banks help to empower them with some of that knowledge. Lots of the local micro-finance institutions do this outreach during the borrower's group meetings or in the branch. Some have required courses they take before securing a loan. They also teach budgeting, finance skills, and savings, all things that can be passed on to the next generation and have a sustainable impact versus things like shoes that are going to wear out.

According to the National Philanthropic Trust, in 2014, Americans gave $359.36 billion to various charities, both in this country and around the world. The average household contribution is $2,974. I wonder what that amount of money given as micro-loans could do.

Unfortunately, since I have been in these second- and third-world countries, I now better understand how terrorism organizations might look like a great opportunity. Looking at the value proposition to local villages from organizations like Hezbollah or ISIS is compelling, given their circumstances.

These groups offer the villagers food, to repair their homes, or to build a shelter and private schools for their children. If you were the father of a starving family and were told if you join their organization and fight that your family will be taken care of, would you enroll? Keep in mind this father is more than likely starving as well, so by joining, he will be fed too. Also, keep in mind they are not presenting themselves as terrorist organizations when they recruit.

ISIS says its mission is to promote freedom of expression, freedom of thought and belief, freedom of intellectual and scientific inquiry, freedom of conscience and religion, including the freedom to change one's religion or belief, and freedom from religion, the freedom not to believe in any deity. After hearing that, and if you didn't know the stories that we know, you would probably think it is a worthy cause to join. As happy, fat Americans we cannot conceive why these people do what they do. When you put it in this context, it begins to make sense to me. As a boy, and less frequently, a girl, you are in a poor area with no access to education. Because your father fights for Hezbollah, you get to go to a private school owned and run by Hezbollah.

As the father, you are grateful because you are giving your family the chance to have more opportunities than you had as a child. By the way, what thoughts do you think are being poured into these children's minds at these private schools? Do you think they are raising a nation of people with radical ideas that could have a profound negative impact on the world for decades to come?

The father who joins now has a well-fed, sheltered, and educated family. Soon, this father or brother will have to make a decision, one that was deliberately not talked about in the initial offer of help. Now that you are in debt to ISIS or Hezbollah, you are given a choice with a couple of options.

Option one: Strap a bomb on your back and go do a terrible deed. Yes, you will die, but your family will be taken care of, and you will go down in history as a hero or martyr.

Option two: Refuse. Then, not only will your family not be fed, sheltered or education, but they, and you, will probably be tortured, raped, and killed.

In ISIS and Hezbollah's minds, they are only killing rich people who are trying to take away their people and suppress their nation. These radical groups are based on fear, intimidation and preying on the uneducated. We have an opportunity to help, empower, and feed these people so that they do not have to make these decisions. It is crucial that these people are looked after so that they do not fall into the wrong hands.

I think there are two different paradigms that are going to happen. One is an exponential growth curve of terrorism. Meaning there will be a J shaped curve on a chart. There has been more terrorism in the last 10 years than in the last 20. There has been more terrorism in the last five years than in the last ten, etc. If you look at the current trajectory if we stay on this pace, it will destroy the world one day. The other exponential growth curve could be love and respect, which will save the world.

Clean Water

Another critical issue in second- and third-world countries is having clean water. I have seen people walking and hiking for hours to get water. I have also seen them hiking to gather wood to burn for cooking because they do not have electricity. There are so many negative issues about these customs.

One, the woman is not able to have a business or earn an income because she spends her entire day collecting water to drink and wood to burn, boiling the water, and cooking. Two, terrible pollution results from the soot generated by all the wood that's being burned. Three, the children who are living in these small homes and are breathing in that smoke suffer the most. By doing something as simple as providing electricity, we can provide people with water. We can provide them with cooking stoves. It is so critical that we get people electricity and well water. There are some great organizations out their working on some amazing solar options to try and address these issues.

Giving Grows

Can you count how many seeds are in an apple? Yes. However, you cannot count how many apples are in a seed. While this is simple, you don't know the impact that we will have in investing in others. We never know if we are going to be the one to change a person's trajectory in life. When I die, I can't take what I have, but I can live in others through what I gave.

As you and those around you give, it pushes us all to give more. It is fun to see children react as you give. I think it is our responsibility as parents to teach our children to give so that they can understand how they can help people. We should also teach them to be humble in their giving. We are not called to be recognized for serving others.

Giving also makes us feel good. Many studies show that people who are given $20 at the beginning of the day with instructions to spend it before day's end feel much more rewarded when they gave it to someone who needed it more than they did.

Many people give for the wrong reasons: because they want to be applauded or rewarded; but that is not the right way to give. The greatest gift is giving to someone knowing that you cannot be repaid. I also encourage you to do your homework before deciding on which organizations to choose. Many waste money on administrative fees. Many are vague about how much of your money actually gets to the people you are trying to help. Today's standard for a top charity is to use no more than 33% of its donations for overhead and administrative costs.

Wondering how your charity measures up? Charity Navigator (http://www.charitynavigator.org/) provides a wealth of information and a rating system on more than 8,000 American charities. Here are three of the most well-known:

- The American Red Cross spends 90.3% of its income on programs and services it delivers to the community.
- Save the Children disburses 90.1% of its donations to programs that benefit children in the United States and around the world.
- Doctors Without Borders uses 87.4% of its funds to provide medical help throughout the world.
- For contrast, some like Children's Charity Fund only gets 17.53% to the base they say they are serving.

Find out what works best for you. Maybe it is giving money; maybe it is giving time, or maybe it's even giving knowledge. People get so caught up on thinking giving means to give money or assets. What other things do you have that you can bless others' lives with?

One of my favorite quotes that my mentor Marshall Thurber says is, "Givers get." I truly believe that in the end, the givers, by helping others, will ultimately achieve their goals. Because of my giving heart and outlook, if I needed a favor or help from anyone, I am sure there are always people who will be willing to help because they have either received from me or they have seen me give to others.

We make a living by what we get. We make a life by what we give.

~ Winston Churchill

CHAPTER TEN
YOUR ABUNDANT FUTURE

Here's to the crazy ones. The misfits. The rebels. The trouble-makers. The round pegs in the square holes. The ones who see things differently. They're not fond of rules. And they have no respect for the status quo. You can quote them, disagree with them, glorify, or vilify them. About the only thing you can't do is ignore them. Because they change things. They push the human race forward. And while some may see them as the crazy ones, we see genius. Because the people who are crazy enough to think they can change the world, are the ones who do.

~ Rob Siltanen

I almost titled this book *The Abundance Affect,* because I think it is key to understand the theory before you can create abundance. The *affect* of abundance starts by being conscious of your thoughts and actions. That creates the *effect*, the results of your emotions, actions, or reactions.

In writing this book, my prayer has been that your future will be filled with abundance, love, joy, peace, patience, kindness, goodness, and self-control.

The Bible verse, John 10:10 says, *"The thief comes only to steal and kill and destroy. I came that they may have life, and have it abundantly."* The key to abundance is meeting limited circumstances with unlimited thoughts. We must become aware of the true power within ourselves. We also have to be aware of the power we may give to others who want to control our lives.

Happiness, love, and abundance are all contagious. So are anger, sadness, and scarcity. You have the choice of which emotions you spread in life. One of the most abundant emotions in the world is love.

Love is as vast as the ocean. No matter how much you take out, you'll never be able to see a drop in the water level. The more you share, the more there is to give. I envision love as one candle lighting thousands of other candles. No matter how many are lit off the one candle, the light from that candle does not diminish. A small flame may not shed much light, but when you share the flame and then put all the flames together, it creates a force for change because it makes each individual flame burn stronger. Share your love.

Here are 10 tips to creating an abundant future:

1. **Live with love in your heart.** I believe that love is the most abundant treasure in the world. It is free and requires nothing more than to be given away. The more love you give, the bigger it grows. It's the one commodity that never depreciates.

2. **Practice the abundant mindset every day.** The energy we expend is the energy we attract. Wake up with gratitude for something, even opening your eyes, each morning. Adopt the *everything is perfect* outlook.

3. **Train yourself to recognize the scarcity mindset in yourself.** It's easy to spot negative behaviors in someone else. Turn that ability inward and begin to eliminate those traits in you.

4. **Write down your vision and work the steps to achieving it.** Do the spreadsheet exercise to discover where you

waste time. Create your one-to-three vital priorities. Make a plan, and work on it every day.

5. **Surround yourself with the right people.** Remember, the right people are those who have the skills and traits you lack and who will speak to you honestly. They also share your beliefs and values.

6. **Turn off technology, and enjoy face-to-face time with your friends and family.** Live in the present, not through the TV, your phone, or the Internet.

7. **Give abundantly.** Whether you volunteer, help a neighbor, care for a family member, or donate to charity, give what you can with an open heart.

8. **Share your knowledge.** Hoarding your skills and ideas can set you up for failure. Share your knowledge with others. It's better to have 80% of a profitable business than 100% of a failed one.

9. **Create an abundant environment for your children.** Teach your children the value of learning. Listen to them. Give them age-appropriate choices, and foster courage and kindness in them.

10. **Choose an abundant life.** Anything you choose to believe will become your truth. Choose to believe in yourself, and believe that your life is going to be full of abundant blessings. Make them happen with intention, focus, and work.

Change is not easy, but you *can* change. Success comes from hard work, making mistakes, and doing more hard work. Practice does make us (if not perfect) better, smarter, and more self-confident.

Working through your issues, creating a new product, or starting a new business are not easy either, but you can do it. You already have the power to succeed within you.

The Abundance Effect does not end when you finish reading this book. My vision for you is that what I've just shared will open your mind to thinking differently and to catching yourself when you fall into negativity. Most of all, I hope you now have the tools to meet any challenge and the confidence to go after your every dream, however wild.

About the Author

Justin has had an extremely successful career in entrepreneurship, particularly real estate. He has built a portfolio of investments that now includes manufacturing, oil and gas, and mortgages, as well as his real estate interest. Justin believes and often teaches topics related to business growth, financial freedom, entrepreneurship, passive income, mindset, and motivation. He currently lives with his wife and two daughters in Fort Collins, Colorado.